PHOENIX

PHOENIX

RISING FROM ADDICTION

Alexa Giebink

A Memoir of Mary Ann Giebink

Mary Ann Gaehle

Forgiveness is the ultimate form of love
–Anonymous

Lee Gaehle

CONTENTS

PART I

My Uncle Don

PART II

The Rise and Fall of Mary Ann

PART III

We Rise From the Ashes

Preface

Yes, this is another addiction story. Fortunately, for my family and me, it is largely a success story. It is a story that includes crime, murder, suicide, betrayal and pain. It is also a story that includes love and courage and perseverance.

My mom is a recovering alcoholic. This is the story of how our family went through hell and back during my grade school years. Ever since my mom sobered up, I have wanted to write our story down so that we could share it with others. Addiction, whether it is to drugs, alcohol, gambling or any other vice, is a common problem in many homes. Addicts and their family members often feel alone which makes it harder to cope with the situation. But they are not alone and I want people to know it is possible to overcome. I hope my family's story gives you hope. And I hope the lessons we have learned will help you deal with whatever adversity you face in your life. All of the events in the following pages are true, although some names have been changed to protect the privacy of those involved.

One summer when I was 21, I was finally given the push I needed to take on this project. My mom, Mary Ann, my dad, Brad, my brother, Jacob, my grandma, Margaret and my boyfriend, Adam, were extremely helpful and cooperative throughout the whole process. I'd like to thank them and Melanie Brown who encouraged me to make it happen. Also I'd like to thank Kyle Vanderberg at KCV Photography for his cover design. The photograph was taken near my childhood home in the intersection where my mom crashed her car during her second DWI and literally hit rock bottom. Through writing this book I have better understood my family, addiction and myself. Although I had to write it rather quickly before I returned to college for my senior year, I poured my heart into this book and I hope you learn and enjoy.

PART I

My Uncle Don

Donald Galland

1
Growing Up Too Fast

I am starting the story with Donald, my uncle. He died in 1991, two years before I was born. His life and death had a major impact on my mom. To understand her struggle, I need to try and understand Don's tragedy.

When Don was born his dad, Robert, was in Vietnam for the Army. My mom remembers seeing newsreels of soldiers fighting and looking for her father. In reality his job was not on the front lines but supervising construction projects, such as gas pipelines. When Robert returned home to South Dakota, initially Don would have nothing to do with him. He didn't know his own dad. Rather quickly a relationship formed but it was a rocky start.

Don was eight years younger than my mom, the youngest in a family of five children. My grandma, Margaret, says he always wanted to grow up too fast. In grade school he would ask to tag along on his brother's dates. She would try to explain that he needed to wait his turn but she often received polite refusal in response.

Before the massive publicity from his criminal offense, Don made the newspaper for several positive events. One day he was walking home by a local college track, which is now the football stadium, and a man on the track collapsed from a heart attack. Don gave him CPR until the ambulance came, saving his life.

In high school Don was a member of the Washington High School drama club. Always the patron of the arts he was seen dressing up as Big Bird and walking in the first Holiday Parade. My grandma still has a copy of the newspaper article that shows Don smiling happily with Big Bird feet on. Also during his one semester at college in Mankato for art, he asked a local company if he could touch up a large Coca-Cola advertisement on the side of their brick building. There is a large article in the local paper with a picture of Don enjoying a refreshing Coke while sitting on his scaffolding.

For a long time all I knew about my uncle was that he was an artist. His portraits and sketches hung on the walls of my relatives' houses. Now his drawing of Albert Einstein hangs above my bookcase. Even in prison he designed stationery with beautiful roses and detailed motorcycles. As I was growing up, there was a wall of shelves in my grandma's basement that held boxes and boxes of this stationery. I had no idea until recently that Don drew it in prison. While in prison he also designed cards for churches. He worked in the print shop in prison before it closed. It gives me some comfort to know he was still able to create while confined.

Success is a large part of our society and our family. For many the pressure can be unbearable. Instead of forming a person into a diamond it can shatter them. Success can be defined in many ways. Are you successful if you're happy and healthy? Are you successful if you make a difference in the world or make a lot of money? By the time Don was in college all of his siblings were leading successful, professional lives. His mother said he was smart but his schooling didn't show it. Don didn't want to put the time in to being successful. Maybe this is why he robbed a pizza restaurant in high school. He couldn't wait to be rich and successful like his siblings. Don later explained that many of his life problems went back to money.

In 1988 Don was 20 and had already dropped out of Mankato State University when he robbed the grocery store. As I write this I am about the same age my uncle was when he made a decision that changed

Encore

The paint that refreshes

The Mankato City Council finally has allowed MSU art major Don Galland to finish his renovation of the Coca-Cola sign painted on the wall of the Stelter Sewing Service building in Mankato's Old Town. Last fall, his work abruptly was halted because the renovation violated a 1972 city code stating that ad signs may not be painted directly on any exterior building surface. The question: Is the repainting an advertising or an historical renovation? The answer: Historical. Once again, Coca-Cola Bottling Co. of Mankato hired Galland to restore the painting. Galland last fall expressed the desire also to restore other wall signs in Mankato, including Pepsi, Mission Orange and 7up. (Right) Galland enjoys a soft drink supplied free of charge by, of course, Coca-Cola. (Below, left) With brush in hand and concentration in mind, Galland paints in details. (Below, right) The MSU artist uses a paint roller to outline the letters.

photos by Mani Boniek

Donald in the Mankato newspaper for restoring the Coca-Cola mural

the rest of his life. One could say it essentially ended his life. I wish sometimes I could snap my fingers and be successful. I let my mind slip to wonder how great it would be to skip the work and worry of securing safety and happiness. It's impossible to know what was racing through Don's head at that time. I don't know the amount of pressure he was under.

I know my grandparents, Don's parents, as loving and supportive. I know that my grandpa, who has passed, and my grandma, who is still alive, value education and bettering yourself. Did Don feel he wasn't living up to their expectations or to society's expectations? Was he simply impatient or misguided as to how to achieve success? I can only wonder. From a letter he wrote it sounds as if his parents were loving and supportive in every way. He never blamed them for his actions.

As far as I know there isn't a key to success. At least one has never been given to me. Success is subjective and personal. It is not something a person should stress over. Unfortunately, I'm afraid that is what Don did. His siblings were 'successful' in their careers whether as a lawyer, in the Army or in the world of big business. They were far from him in age and often geography. Don wanted to achieve the same success as his siblings. This caused him stress, which drove him to unthinkable action.

Two years after Don had robbed the pizza place he had only paid $250 out of the $3,100 owed in restitution. My mom, a lawyer, had found out there were warrants issued for Don's arrest because of checks written for his restitution that came back with insufficient funds. She told him about the warrants and he decided it was time to leave town. On his way out he stopped to pick up a soda at a neighborhood grocery store owned by Jim and Sarah Peterson*, a husband and wife. Inside he saw the cash register drawer filled with cash and he decided this was his way out of town. Immediately he pulled a gun on Sarah demanding the cash while Jim was downstairs.

---

* Names have been changed to protect their privacy.

2
111 One-Dollar Bills

Don quickly realized the storeowner could describe and identity him.
Maybe the authorities would be able to figure out who he was. He
took Sarah to the back room and shot her in the back of the head.
Unfortunately in these situations, little attention is given to the
victims. The following is what I know about the couple from the
newspaper articles.

The couple had been married for six years. Jim was older, 58, and
this was his second marriage. His second wife, Sarah, was 27 when she
passed away. Seven years before Jim buried his wife, he'd had to bury
a son he had lost to Hodgkin's disease. Sarah's friends and family said
she had led a quiet, unassuming life. The marriage meant everything
to Sarah. The couple did everything together, including running the
neighborhood grocery store. Sarah enjoyed swimming in their back-
yard pool but her friends and relatives said there was nothing she liked
more than being Jim's wife.

In the articles, friends and family have a hard time understanding
why such as thing occurred. Sarah's mother is quoted as saying, "I
can't understand. It's just…she has so much to live for. And now she's
gone." I'm writing this book to try and understand the circumstances
that have shaped my family but there is no making sense of why it

all happened the way it did. The gravity of the tragedy for her family could never be fully expressed.

Jim seemed to try and move on as much as he could. One article reports him opening his grocery store again. It has a large picture of Jim standing behind the counter where he last saw his wife alive. He is wearing a wedding ring she had meant to give him that Christmas. That fateful night he was going to be working in the basement and he kidded Sarah about being quiet. They both said I love you.

Jim said Sarah would have wanted him to reopen up the store. She would have said, "You can't pay the bills if the doors are locked." Tragedy again struck just over a month after his wife was killed when Jim was found dead in his garage. He was sitting in his Jeep with the garage door closed. The cause of death was carbon monoxide poisoning, but it was ruled neither an accident nor a suicide.

Jim's mother-in-law was firm that it was not suicide. She is quoted as saying, "I can't believe he took his life. I know he didn't. I know damn well he didn't take his own life." Jim had heart issues and appeared sick before his death. Also there were bruises on his hands as if he had tried to get out of the vehicle. She said he hadn't been taking his appropriate medication after the death of his wife. A friend of Jim's suggested he had a heart attack but it still made no sense that the garage door was shut if he was intending on backing out of the garage.

Jim's mother-in-law said that he was loved and supported by friends and her family. Regardless Jim certainly must have suffered. He had lost his son to cancer and his other son quit talking to him after he had divorced his first wife, the boy's mother. He had two grandchildren in Washington, D. C. whom he had never met. The love of his second wife must have been a relief from the loneliness. The loss of his wife may have been too much to bear. Although Don was never charged with Jim's death, he always felt he had two deaths on his hands.

After shooting Sarah Peterson, that December night, my uncle left the store in a panic with only 111 one-dollar bills. He knew he had done something horrific. After driving around in a daze, instead of high-tailing out of town, he was discovered in a residential neighborhood where cops quickly circled his car. Still inside, Don shot himself in the neck barely missing the main veins.

My grandpa was at a hospital for back surgery that night and my grandmother was with him. They saw pictures and video of Don and his car on the ten o'clock news with no names given at first. They recognized his tennis shoes and his height by his feet hanging over the gurney. It followed that he had been arrested for murder. Then my grandparents heard the news for the second time from a woman who came into their room.

That night my mom came home from league bowling and checked her messages. Her mom had left a couple of messages that didn't give details but my mom could tell something was wrong. She doesn't remember why but she immediately ran to her closet and saw that her gun was missing. Her other brother, John, had given it to her for graduation from law school. Don had stolen the gun and used it to murder Sarah Peterson.

My mom knew her dad was in the hospital so she called his room. My grandma told her that they had seen a news story about Don. He had been arrested for murder. My mom hurried to the hospital to comfort her parents but they were inconsolable. Grandma said nothing was going to be the same ever again and she was right.

Don had been brought to the other hospital in town and my mom went to visit him. He was not only her brother but also her best friend. When she arrived they denied her access. She told them she was an attorney and she was representing him therefore they could not refuse to allow her to see him.

Inside Don was crying. He was extremely upset and repeatedly saying he wanted to die. She told him she would talk to an attorney but all he could say was that he wanted to die. I can't imagine having someone so close to me commit such a violent crime but I know somewhat how my mom felt in that hospital room.

Don had sobbed the words I would hear almost two decades later. When my mom attempted suicide I visited her in the hospital and in front of my father, my brother and me she wailed that she too wanted to die. It's crushing to hear someone so important to you say they want

7

SIOUX VALLEY HOSPITAL

1100 South Euclid Avenue
P.O. Box 5039
Sioux Falls, South Dakota 57117-5039
(605) 333-1000

THE VOICES OF CHILDEN
ARE STRONG IN MY HEAD.
THEIR Laughter makes me smile
THEIR tears make me cry
THE child depends on guidence
~~that~~ A child without that guidence
is lost, HE Swims through his
life without touching the water.
The RIVER Flows endless without
Death and without Birth. WATER
is the stream of life.
When a drop of water enters
the river you can no longer distiquish
it from the others.
It becomes one and as
long as there is a stream, the
drop is never lost. It is always
there in the spirit of the river.

Don Galland
12·10·90

to leave you. It's crushing to see them in such internal pain and agony.

In the process of writing this book, my grandma dug out old papers of Don's. The following is a poem written by Don on Sioux Valley Hospital stationery. It is dated two days after Don shot the woman and himself. There is very little that exists to give insight into what Don was thinking and what he went through during that time. I am not going to try to interpret the words of his poem but let them speak for themselves.

> The voices of children
> Are strong in my head.
> Their laughter makes me smile
> Their tears make me cry
> The child depends on guidance
> A child without that guidance
> Is lost. He swims through his
> Life without touching the water.
> The river flows endless without
> Death and without birth. Water
> Is the stream of life.
> When a drop of water enters
> The river you can no longer distinguish
> It from the others.
> It becomes one and as
> Long as there is a stream, the
> Drop is never lost. It is always
> There in the spirit of the river.
> —Donald Galland
> 12-10-1988

After my mom saw her brother in the hospital room where he later wrote the poem above, she went back to the hospital where her folks were. She told them he was going to recover from the gunshot wound. Then she went home. Allowing a quick shower, my mom rushed to the courthouse to be the maid of honor for her paralegal's wedding.

9

Unable to hold herself up anymore at last she went home and collapsed with grief and exhaustion.

Shortly thereafter my mom gathered the strength to meet with the head of the Public Defender's office. He told her that Don was looking at the death penalty. It was a nightmare coming true. He also told her that there weren't bad people but good people who did bad things. This was comforting to her and helped her to understand the situation a little better.

It was all so shocking, especially to my grandparents. Don was always good to them. He never sassed back or swore at them. They couldn't understand how a person can act so differently in different situations. He had never been violent before. It is easy to vilify criminals when you have no relation to them. How do wrap your mind around a relative and friend you love murdering someone? Grandpa held it in and cried. It hurt, as it should. It is only human.

When he was in jail before being sentenced, Don tried to slit his wrists with a razor. My mom and her parents were not notified of the suicide attempt. When my mom went to see him a few days later, he became very angry. He thought they had been told and simply didn't care. My mom cared so much. It hurt more because there was nothing she could do to help. This guilt and helplessness compounded for years almost certainly contributing to her later addiction and meltdown.

Many in the justice system pushed for the death penalty for Don. At that time no one had been given the death penalty in South Dakota since 1947. The rumor was that the State's Attorney was looking to make his career on the case by pushing for the death penalty. He supposedly wanted the publicity so he could run for another political office. From the newspaper articles it appears that the case received a lot of press and attention. Don was charged with both the act of murder and premeditated murder. This resulted in two murder counts. The pre-meditated murder charge carried the possibility of the death penalty.

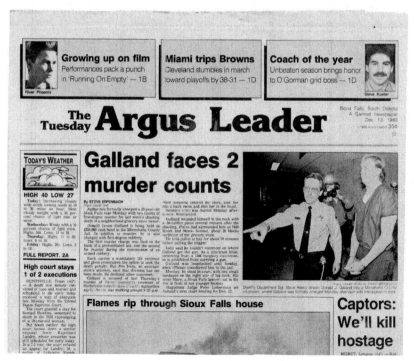

11

The newspaper polled a few members of the local community on whether Don should receive the death penalty. Three out of the five believed no, he should not be put to death. One argument was based around the idea that life is sacred. The death penalty tends to be more about revenge than justice. Also some argued that the chance of killing an innocent person with the death penalty is too high to risk. One man is quoted as saying, "He took a life, he should suffer for it…but I can't figure out where they got premeditated murder." What he and many others didn't understand was that it was classified as premeditated because Don took the gun into the back room. It is considered premeditated murder even if the premeditation happens just three seconds before the act. This explanation of premeditated murder was unclear or absent in the newspapers.

On the reverse side, the other two people polled supported the death penalty. One woman was even a friend of Don's. She said that if someone takes a life, it is only fair that they give up theirs. The other man said that too many criminals had been 'getting off' after committing violent crimes. One must assume he believes that life without parole is 'getting off.'

In his motion hearing Don surprised many by jumping up and pleading guilty to the act of murder charge, which didn't carry the death penalty. The lawyers did the best they could. They argued that his guilty plea would bar further prosecution for the premeditated murder charge thus escaping the possibility of the death penalty. Some who supported the death penalty argued that Don shouldn't have been given the option, or a way out of the death penalty. But the State's Attorney, who was pushing for the death penalty, decided not to appeal the case and let it rest. An editorial supported this decision saying that often these decisions are driven by emotions and other factors outside of state law. The author of the editorial believed a pursuit of the death penalty after Don's plea would have been excessive. One of Don's lawyers is quoted as saying, "Enough people have died. I don't think any purpose is served by killing a kid. Legally, we hope we've saved his life."

Because Don pled guilty to the murder charge, the judge sentenced him to life without parole. He was 21. Essentially a kid. In South

Galland pleads guilty

Surprise move brings him life sentence

By TODD NELSON
Argus Leader Staff

Donald James Galland surprised prosecutors Friday when he pleaded guilty to one count of felony murder and was sentenced to life in prison without parole, taking an unexpected legal risk that could save his life.

Defense lawyers argued that Galland's guilty plea would bar further prosecution on a premeditated murder charge for which he faces the death penalty if convicted.

Prosecuting Galland on that charge would violate constitutional provisions that protect a person from twice being put in jeopardy for the same offense, defense lawyer Michael Schaffer said Friday.

"My research indicates that the counts of premeditated murder and felony murder are the same offense," Schaffer said. "Mr. Galland has pleaded guilty and received a life sentence for felony murder and cannot be prosecuted for premeditated murder. In my opinion, this thing should be over."

Circuit Judge R.D. Hurd declined to rule Friday on a defense motion to prevent the state from seeking the death penalty on the premeditated murder charge or dismiss that count and the remaining charges. He scheduled a hearing on the motion for May 30.

"If the court agrees with us, we've saved a kid's life today," said lawyer Michael Butler, who assisted in Galland's defense.

Galland faces two first-degree murder charges and a first-degree robbery charge in connection with the Dec. 8, shooting death of Sioux Falls grocery store clerk murder charges during an armed robbery in

Galland/See 2A

Deputy Sheriff Steve Reecy (left), escorts Donald Galland back to the Public Safety Building on Friday after Galland was sentenced to life in prison without parole.

Argus Leader photo by DIANE DULTMEIER

Dakota, life is life. He would never be released. So Don pled guilty to murder to secure his life and the certainty that he would go to the penitentiary. It could seem somewhat ironic that two years later he made the decision to take his life.

Don (middle) in prison. One day a motorcycle was brought in. Motorcycles were big in our family.

3
How Does it Feel?

My grandparents visited Don twice a week in prison. Before he was imprisoned, they used to travel a lot, touring the country on their BMW motorcycle. Grandma said she wouldn't leave town because she didn't want to miss her two visits with Don every week. In continuity with her philosophy, my grandma recalls that they never talked about what happened. They knew he knew he did something terribly wrong but the topic was never brought up. The discussion was always focused on his daily routine and wellbeing.

Although Don didn't talk to his parents about what he had done, he talked to my mom, his best friend. My mom, who went to the prison to see clients, saw him often. She says he was very remorseful and guilt-stricken. Since Jim Peterson, the husband of the woman he murdered, later allegedly killed himself, Don always felt he was to blame for two deaths.

Although Don was in prison for life, he didn't cease to exist. Here are some of the events from the three years he spent behind bars. In prison Don was an easy target. He had a lot of resources since his family was there for him and provided him with money. For example he had a subscription to the newspaper, which he could trade for other objects in prison. People would always try to con him out of things or simply assault him for whatever it was they wanted. At one point he was hit from behind with some object, breaking his jaw and destroying his dental work. The assailant then stole some of Don's possessions.

When Don was in jail, there was a yearly banquet called Lifers Banquet where family members could have a meal with sons, brothers and husbands who were incarcerated for life. My mom attended one year and didn't expect it to be as long as it was. She had somewhere to be but couldn't leave. Don wittily remarked, "How does it feel?"

At one point Don wanted my mom to smuggle in pot for him. She had been introduced to pot by a boyfriend whom she had met at a party rather early on in life and was the first person to get Don high when they were younger. But at this point, her reaction was, "You ruined your life and now you want to ruin mine?" Whether she said that out loud or not, she refused to bring him drugs. Instead he had someone empty a highlighter and fill it with marijuana and then send it into the prison. She said he shouldn't be doing that, and he replied, "What are they going to do, take away my birthday?"

Back then prisoners could have a lot of stuff in their cells. Don even had a box cutter, surprisingly. He had a large collection of art supplies, which enabled him to draw the stationery mentioned above. The Einstein drawing I have was drawn in 1989 while he was in jail. Unfortunately, at one point there was a riot and everything was thrown away or sent out to relatives.

Most of the guys in prison came from small towns in South Dakota, and many of them couldn't read or write. Don wrote letters for at least one man, but made him copy the letters so he could at least try to learn how to read and write. According to my mom, he would never ask what they did to end up incarcerated. Although Don felt that he made no contribution in prison, it sounds like he still led a somewhat productive and helpful life.

After the verdict and sentencing, Don had told my mom he would not last five more years after the murder. He did not want to live that way, in prison. Three and a half years later, two years before I was born, he hung himself and died. The last time my mom saw Don she was at the prison

Mary Ann, Don and Margaret Galland, my Grandma, at the "Lifers Banquet" where families could join inmates incarcerated for life.

Margaret and Mary Ann at Don's funeral.

In Memory Of

DONALD JAMES GALLAND

February 16, 1968
November 8, 1991

The souls of the just are in the hands of God. They seemed, in the view of the foolish, to be dead, but they are in peace.

Precious in the eyes of the Lord is the death of His faithful one.

———

BARNETT-LEWIS
FUNERAL HOME

to visit a client and told her brother she didn't have time to visit with him. My mom felt that it might have hastened the suicide because he might have interpreted it as my mom not caring very much about him.

More than sixty people were at his funeral in the penitentiary. At that point it was the biggest funeral the prison had seen in living memory. There was also another funeral at a church for friends and family. He was very well liked and is still missed very much.

My grandma recalls receiving a phone call from Don shortly before he died. He asked her if she still had his suit…and she didn't think anything of it. She was so busy with her daily routine she didn't stop to wonder about a strange question. She thought perhaps he was reminiscing.

My mom got the call in the middle of the night. She called a friend to come over and comfort her. She and her parents went to the hospital to see Don for the last time, to see that he was gone. Don had said that in some ways, his death would be a release for them, that they wouldn't have to be chained to the prison with him. Of course my mom would rather him be alive and she thinks he would have had a chance to get out at some point but in a way it was a release from the worry and some of the pain.

The hospital inquired whether the family wanted to donate his organs. After they were harvested the hospital said they were not going to use them because he had been in prison. The fact that they rejected Don's healthy organs and the fact that they harvested them anyway really upset his mom. My mom was a member at the Lion's Club, which had just started the eye bank. Through them they were able to use his corneas for two people without. Because of Don, two people were able to see and that gave my mom comfort after the organ insult.

My family had a variety of reactions to Don's criminal offense and death. My grandpa held it in as men were often taught to do, or naturally do. In general the family didn't talk about it. I believe talking helps but who really knows how to handle a situation like that. Everyone copes and heals in different ways. Grandpa was hurt. He kept the pain inside. Crying was the only external manifestation of his suffering.

Don's siblings had regrets. My uncle John told my grandmother that he should have spent more time with Don. My grandma explained that

19

it wasn't his fault. There were ten years between John and Don. That was not something he should worry about. My mom's then sister-in-law who was married to her brother Louis said she always admired how the family stood by Don. My mom didn't even consider another option. The three siblings, besides my mom, all lived out of state so they were distanced from the situation in some respect. My grandma remembers that everyone was polite to Don, and that he was not abused or neglected by anyone in their family.

My grandma's philosophy toward the whole situation was simple. It was Don's choice, not her fault, and a person has to move on. In general she didn't believe in talking about it, like my grandpa. She says it would have been difficult to talk about it, which is natural. The public didn't bother them because they knew it was a difficult and closed subject. Bringing up the sensitive topic before one has time to heal would be like pouring salt on a wound. Now that more time has passed, it stings less.

Although people didn't openly discuss Don's crime with his family, gossip was particularly painful during the healing process. Gossip sometimes appears as news articles and comment sections that are used to satisfy the public's craving for the ugly details. People are vicious and ignorant in their attacks. For them it must be a thrill and they attack before ever bothering to know all the facts. They care little or not at all about the real people that are affected by the tragedy. Criminals have families and friends who all must live with their relative's or friend's mistakes. I experienced this first hand when my mom negatively made the news repeatedly.

Gossip can also appear in its traditional form as chatter between people. For some reason there is an inherent curiosity in humans that draws people to the drama. In the world some people are there to support and others want to be entertained. I have learned how important true support is and how harmful people are who are in it for the drama.

Excluding gossip, it is healthy to let the pain out and to talk so that one can begin to understand and accept what has happened. This was the best way for my grandma to accept that life happens and it was no use to blame herself or others. No one else was guilty of Don's crime.

Although she didn't talk much about Don's situation in everyday life, my grandma did talk about it in specific situations. After Don's death, my grandma was encouraged by her priest to meet with other ladies who had relatives in prison. She would often travel with the priest to churches and gyms to share her story and her struggle in order to raise money for the priest's prison ministry.

She would have the audience, packed in the space, in the palm of her hands. That is easy to imagine as the story still captivates me even after two decades have passed. The following speech includes some of the facts and details. It also shows my grandmother's emotions, often anger, and that she was trying to make sense of the impossible situation. A woman approached my grandma after her speech one time and told her that now she knew what her mother had gone through. Her mother's son, the woman's brother, was currently in prison. I hope this book has the same effect now that my grandma's speech did then.

Never in my life did I ever believe our family would share a severe crisis. It was tough love with Donald, our son. My husband was in the hospital for back surgery. I stayed late one evening. On the ten o'clock news, they told of a young man who shot and killed a woman. The TV station showed a man we recognized as our son. He was 6 foot 5 inches so his feet hung over the stretcher. We could see it was his jeans and shoes. We didn't see his face. Before the police could get control of Donald, he shot himself in the neck. He wanted to kill himself. You are in shock and the fear of the unknown begins. I know I cried the whole night. What could we do, how do you tell the brothers and sisters? It also was our oldest daughter's birthday. My son was expecting their second child that month. Too many things were happening. Our son's life was a mess. What do you do? It was real. The TV and papers were digging up all they could about Donald, what school he attended, picture, and so forth. Who should I be angry at? Donald—he was young and knew right from wrong.

The next day the authorities did grant me 15 minutes with my son. I couldn't hold him, touch him, only talk to him in the hospital. His arm did extend on the bed, so I touched his fingers. I asked him how he felt, his answer was, "I'm all mixed up." My mind was, what could I do? He was in someone else's hands. We both knew what an awful thing it was for him to do.

When he was well enough to leave the hospital, he went to the jail. After three months, he attempted suicide. On the day we were to visit, he was angry. He was surprised no one had told us what he had done to his wrist and arm. We saw the many stitches he had. Again, we were angry. He was angry at us. When he was thinking right, he still believed we could perform miracles for him. Many times we had to tell him, it was all out of our hands. He was young and this could not be fixed.

Somehow you do keep your sanity and you do worry. You again realize what all he must go through. The lawyers were good to Donald. They asked us many questions. How would they help him? I was concerned that they would not treat him like a person. My son later admitted a guilty plea and was sentenced to life in prison. At the age of 21 spending the rest of his life in prison was a reality I almost could hardly think about and he must have felt how unbelievable it was for him. You can't hide. You do suffer through it.

In prison, he worked in the print shop for a few months. One fellow in the print shop and Donald didn't get along. Let's say they had a communication gap. One morning he decided to let Donald know his real feelings and hit him in the jaw with a 2 by 4, broke his jaw. Donald couldn't tell who did it. One doesn't admit something like that in prison. Donald spent three days in the hospital. We were not allowed to see him. The prison had guards with him at the hospital. To this day, it is hard for me to accept. They have their rules. Of course, I was angry again. It was not easy to see his name in the paper and on TV. Donald filed bankruptcy. Again his name appeared on the front page. You do lose friends, yet I found out some people are not your friends. One lady told me, I know how you feel. My answer was, no, you don't. I cared about Donald and that he keep his sanity in prison. He did like to draw. I would get paper, paints and brushes so he would have the supplies to do what he enjoyed doing.

My husband and I would visit him as much as we were allowed. I would even dress up and wear jewelry. I know I needed to feel good, be in a good mood and be comfortable in an unpleasant environment. I couldn't let Donald down. He was always happy to see us. He put on a happy face so I had to do the same.

Almost three years later, Donald did commit suicide in prison. He left two notes telling his brothers and sisters how he felt about them and loved them all, each in a different way. Donald wanted to end the suffering and help everyone get on with their lives. There were so many things we didn't talk about. That past was gone and he was young.

This group of friends helped us with our anger. We needed to sort out so many frustrations. There are people who do understand and you can talk to them. You do become a survivor. You find the strength through prayer. You even search for the right prayers. I have many. God does hear us. You are a survivor and I am a survivor.

—Margaret

When I read this speech for the first time, still on typewriter paper, I was surprised at the extent of the anger she felt. It's hard for me to imagine my grandma angry, but she went through extraordinary circumstances. She has mentioned to me that many of those at church were only interested in the gossip. Because of this, my mom tells me, my grandma pulled away from the church, which she had been very dedicated to. However, her personal faith helped her through, as did talking to professionals and sharing with others who had experienced a tragedy. She is a survivor. We all have survived and we will continue to survive. Be fortified in the knowledge that you can make it through and come out even stronger.

My grandma has been a big influence on me. I know her as a strong and independent woman. In middle school I essentially moved in with her because the new school I had transferred to was only ten blocks from her house. I was not allowed to cry in her house. Although crying can be healthy, as my mom taught me, I believe my grandma's message was a good one. She taught me that no matter what it is, I can get through it and that it is up to me to determine how my life turns out.

Twenty years ago my grandma didn't talk about Don but she opened up for me as I was writing this book. No tears fell but she said it was hard. I could see it in her eyes. It was as if she was staring into the past and remembering. Regardless she said I could ask her anything. Maybe she realizes now that talking about it can help. It can help her and my mother heal and it can also help my brother and me heal from the blowback. Furthermore, this is an opportunity for me to get to know the uncle I never had the pleasure to meet.

Don drew these roses while in prison.

4
Losing Her Best Friend

Out of my family, Don's imprisonment and later death possibly hit my mom the hardest. He was her best friend and confidant. There was no one else in the world she was that close to and she didn't pursue professional help to deal with her deep emotions. My mom had been drinking casually since high school and the drinking escalated in her post college years. A little while before Don died, when my mom was in her late 20s, she went through a six-month outpatient program and was sober for six months afterwards. She knew she had a problem and it was getting worse. This outpatient program staved off her chronic alcoholism. However, Don's death added too much pressure and she went back to drinking. In an interview by a local news station in 2014 my mom stated, concerning Don's death, "At that point, I believe I became a functioning alcoholic. I think that's when it all possibly started."

My mom did what she had to do to sort everything out after his death. She was the strong one for the family and tried to keep it together for everyone else. For a while after the murder, she couldn't get out of bed. My grandma would come over and make her take a shower and go to work. She always felt really guilty constantly asking herself, "What could I have done?"

Because he was her younger brother, she felt a tremendous amount of responsibility for him. She was to be his role model and mentor but she felt she didn't do her job. In regards to the rest of the community she was the one in the spotlight. She had to hold it together. There were days she would be at the courthouse ready to do a case and someone would bring up Don. She couldn't start bawling so she put up a big wall. This wall kept out everyone and she never had another confidant. She never fully trusted anyone else because of her defensiveness and the fear of losing another person.

The experience impeded my mom from further bonding with other people through openly talking and sharing. For years after her brother's death, people unwittingly would ask how he was doing and that would bring the weight of tragedy crushing down again. Instead of healing properly, she focused on overachieving and helping everyone else with their problems. She threw herself into her successful law firm and eventually bonded with alcohol and marijuana instead of her family and friends. Years of dealing with her clients' vicious divorces and representing persons who were guilty also weighed on her. No matter the situation, my mom always felt apart, like an outsider. In public she mastered the art of pretending everything was fantastic. But at home we felt her absence, emotional and physical.

Although my mom had a hard time coping and reaching out, the evidence shows that her siblings supported her in healthy and productive ways. When she was feeling guilty, her brother Louis commented that Don was a train headed for a brick wall and it was not her fault. My mom also said to her sister that the situation builds character. Chloe, her sister, wittily said, "Mary, you have enough character."

Though the general public left my family alone, the media did their job and reported the whole way through. On most occasions they would remark that the criminal was local attorney Mary Galland's brother. She had opened her own law office about a year before that. My grandma was the receptionist and my grandpa was the business manager. My grandpa had mortgaged his BMW car for the business loan so there was a lot at stake. They all struggled for multiple reasons the first few years.

Because of all the media attention, my mom's law office was packed with business. Perhaps people thought that she would understand their situations more since she was so close to the other side of the law. Over time she proved to be very successful. She feels she was good at her job, doing over sixty jury trials in her career and receiving many awards. All the while she was dealing privately with the pain from the loss of her brother, secretly using alcohol and marijuana.

Although it was hard when people would bring up Don after his death, she used those moments to remember him. This happened not too long ago with a friend of Don's girlfriend at the time. In addition, my mom had the same issues with gossip that my grandma did. Everyone wanted to know. When you hear about a person doing something like that you wonder about the rest of their family. You wonder, "What are they like?" or, "Did they create the monster?"

In the aftermath of Don's death, my mom called her ex-boyfriend to let him know what had happened. They had been together for seven years and when she called he said he already knew. He wanted to know the scoop. At that point she told him there was a psychological evalu-ation being done on the family and with his next words he slapped her in the face. He said, "Mental illness runs in the family."

The attention caused by her brother's crime and subsequent suicide directed many people into her law firm, but there were adverse effects for business as well. The judges, particularly the head judge, weren't giving her court appointments. She wrote a letter asking why she was not receiving any appointments and he replied that he was not going to give her a murder case. My mom had just been wondering about misdemeanors.

Murder cases were never on the table. In order to be appointed a murder case you had to do one with someone else first. Most of the profession didn't treat her the same after that, or at least she felt that way. If some in the legal profession and the general public couldn't separate my mom from her brother, how would she have a chance of separating herself from his crime and his guilt?

My mom always felt the penitentiary was liable for Don's suicide. In a harsh coincidence, she'd had a mock trial in law school about a jail suicide. She never thought the circumstances of the mock trial would become so real. The prison building in which Don was incarcerated was built in the late 1800s and has had minimal renovations, which possibly enabled his suicide. Before Don hung himself with his bed sheets from the bars of the cell, he wired the gate shut so that they would have a hard time reaching him.

In an article captioned "Galland commits suicide in prison," the guards claim that they had talked to him twenty minutes before on an hourly routine check, which must have been 2am. Staff members claim that he seemed nervous so they made an unscheduled visit to his cell at 2:25am, when they saw him. They cut him down and gave CPR until the ambulance arrived. Don's heart stopped beating at 12:30pm later that day.

After Don's death, the inmates in the cells next to his wrote my mom. They said that they heard Don suffocating and yelled for help for an hour. Maybe those twenty minutes seemed like an hour to the inmates or maybe the guards did not do their routine check in at 2am. There was also a rumor from the guys next to Don's cell that the guards were selling drugs. They claimed that Don owed them money so the guards let him die. True or not, these thoughts are awful to contemplate.

In the same article, the warden comments that Don had made no other suicide attempts while in the prison. Although that is technically true, there were several previous documented suicide attempts, one while he was being apprehended by the police and one while he was in jail before being moved to prison.

The details of his death don't line up and that gives me as much suspicion as my mom had. But none of the family wanted to go through suing the prison. A lawsuit would not bring Don back. If staff were slacking, hopefully his death would remind them of the importance of their job.

My mom recently worked for an in-patient rehabilitation facility and many staff would not do rounds because it was easy not to. They didn't realize or care about the importance of their job. Real people's lives are on the line. Although the men and women in prison and rehab have made mistakes, they are still human and still have a chance to lead positive and healthy lives.

30

5
In His Own Words

As far as I know, there exists one letter by Don from the time after that dreadful December night. It is dated December 12th, 1989, four days after the murder. It was written before he was sentenced to life in prison and his fate was still undecided. Reading this letter was the first time Don felt like a real person to me. My training in history has taught me to look at old newspaper articles objectively and tell a story based on evidence. But this letter brings him to life. In the letter he tries to make sense of what happened and reminisces about his life.

My uncle writes about people and places very familiar to me. This connects him to the family as I know it and to my life. He comments about my cousins, who had the fortune of meeting him when they were young and visiting him in the penitentiary. From jail he writes about wishing to hug his mom and being unable. I know how great my grandma's hugs are. He writes of the love he received and felt for his family and that comforts me.

The pain and guilt he feels for what he has done and his hope for the future hurts. As I read it I wished for it to all turn out okay for him, but I know it didn't. In one letter I met my uncle and I lost him.

Dear Mom and Dad, and family

Today I go to court and I will have cameras in my face and I will have reporters trying to ask me questions. What has happened is not your fault; it's deep inside me. I've been covering lies with lies since seventh grade and I've developed what I think is a split personality. I need Dad to know that the days I spent with him and you, mom, were the best in my life. I actually felt close to you and I was saying I love you the best that I knew how. One Thursday I lost base with who I am, which had been happening for a long time. I do remember what happened but I don't know why! For reasons you know I can't tell you about what went wrong that night. But I want you to know that there is nothing in the Donald that you raised and that Tammy and Sonja fell in love with that could have done that.

Sonja is going to be a big part in my life and so is Tammy (as a friend). I hope that you will accept them as family friends and Sonja even as more than that. Tammy was a lot to me, as far as, I confided to her almost everything in my life. The only exception that she did not know that I was also engaged to Sonja and we would have been married 12-17-88, this Saturday. Please listen to both of them to help you understand me.

My life's problems have always referred back to money. I am here on this earth today for something but I don't know what. I never gave Jesus or God much of a chance but I feel the good in the air around me. I will soon find out why I'm here. Until then all I can do now is let Jesus lead me to what I hope will be a happy ending. Maybe it will result in being able to be with the people who have showed me that I am worth something and they love me. My family has been disgraced but maybe I can make up for that.

This letter I'm writing is on the <u>drawing tablet</u> that I bought here. Aside from this paper I bought 2 pencils and soap, deodorant, lifesavers and 3 bottles of root beer, envelopes and of course a toothbrush and paste.

My pain has been more and the pills work less. When I left the hospital the doctor said, "when will he be checked" and they told him "Wednesday." Then the doctor said I "should be checked

12-12-88

Dear Mom & Dad & family,

Today I go to court and I will have cameras in my face and I will have reporters trying to ask me questions. What has happen is not your fault it's deep inside me. I've been covering lies with lies since 7th grade and I've developed what I think is a split person-ality. I need Dad to know that the days I spent with him and you mom were the best in my life. I actually felt close to you and I was saying I love you the best that I knew how.   one thursday I lost base with who I am which had been happening for along time. I do remember what happen but I don't know why! for Reasons you know I can't tell you about what went wrong that night. But I want you to know that there is nothing in the Donald that you raised and that Tammy & Sonja fell in love with that could have done that. Sonja is going to be a big part in my life and so is Tammy-(as my friend) I hope that you will accept them as family friends and Sonja even as more then that. Tammy was alot to me, as far as, I confied to her almost everything in my life. The only exception that she did not know that I was also engaged to Sonja and we would have been married 12-17-88 this Saterday. Please listen to both of them to help you understand me. My lifes problems have always referred back to money. I am here on this before that." But they just told me now it will be on Wednesday. It's hard to move except for the first hour after I take my pill. My right eye has been affected by my injury along with the movement of my right hand and arm. At least I've been able to write because this has kept me sane.

Mom, I started a journal as of 12-11 and I've found great release and strength in doing this and being able to write down every thought. I'm in solitary confinement, it's silent here most of the time but if I listen close I can hear the radio in the hallways. I've been hearing some <u>Christ</u>mas music songs and I always think of you, mom. It's your favorite music. So happy and light, it really helps breaks the silence. I just found out it's 9:00pm. Deputy Doug just took me downstairs and got my fingerprints.

It was so nice to hear Chloe's voice on the phone. I hope she's going to be ok. You're probably reading this as well. The cards from Josh and Adam haven't got here yet but I'm really looking forward to receiving them. Oh how I wish I was still that little boy who shared a room with his oldest sis. Did I always try to put my legs on yours? I know when John would come home from college and sleep with me I did that. God how I was looking forward to seeing John. It's been so long and there is so much that I wish I could change about my <u>whole life</u>. Nothing good has come of it at all. I was working on paintings for everyone's Christmas presents but those never got finished. I never did master that airbrush in the past year.

I want everyone to know this wasn't anybody's fault but I do need your love and support to help me get my life back in order. All I want for Christmas is to see my family together forever. It's been 6 years since we had a family picture and all been together for <u>Christ</u>mas. I don't know how you can all still love me but please don't stop, especially now I need you. God, how I wish right now I could have that hug <u>mom</u>! I think I'm having a nervous breakdown or something; I need to get some help with my mind. If I'm not crazy I'm getting there now. I do believe I'm chemically dependent to pot, I don't even know how to spell marjuana (sp). Also in this past month I've done some cocaine. But the time I was with you, dad, I *was straight. When I think back to the time we spent together at the rallies, dad, we were together but yet in our own little worlds. I wish I would have given you more time, you and mom and everyone but I was so consumed by the pot and myself. Now I want to give and I have nothing to give.*

I tried to give Sonja and Tyler all the love I had and she wanted more, as in material things, and now she realizes how much love I was giving. It's not her fault but I want you to love her and Tammy as if they were family. I and Sonja are still praying for that second chance. If I do at some point get to make up for my bad years I want to work with children because their futures should be filled with promise and hope. Maybe I could do some paintings and you can sell them next summer. I've got some great ideas. I don't know what else to write now but I will write more in the morning. I think I get the phone also. I love you ALL!

Donald
P. S. Can I get some <u>pictures</u>!

In the course of writing this book, Don's letter fostered great emotions in me. As I cried over Don's words, my friend asked me why I was doing this. Why was I digging up the painful past and insisting on writing about it? It's a fair question. Ever since my mom was released from prison and has been living a sober healthy life, I've wanted to write our story. For one, it is healthier to talk about it than keep it buried. It helps us all to try to understand how and why it all happened. Second, as long as we keep thinking about and remembering the past, we are less likely to slip back into bad habits and behavior. Lastly and most importantly, I want to share our story with others.

Don was heavily in the newspapers from the day he committed the murder to the day he died. My mom also was in the newspaper throughout her whole career and breakdown. Our story has never been private but has been out in the community since day one. By adding my voice I can help set the record straight where there has often been misinformation. As I mentioned briefly earlier, it is many more times harder to vilify someone you know or are more familiar with. We must never forget that life is complicated and so are people. It's never as simple as it may seem.

I hope those who are reading this learn that there is hope. Whether you need to forgive or be forgiven, it is possible. It is possible to recover and move on from a tragedy. In AA, Alcoholics Anonymous, they say that if you don't forgive you are putting yourself above God because God forgives. I don't know exactly how my family survived Don's incarceration and death and I don't know how my family survived my mom's alcoholism, attempted suicide and incarceration but maybe as I write it out some truths will become evident.

...marijuana... ...in this past month I've done some cocaine. But the time I was with you Dad I was straite. When I think back to the time we spent together at the ralleys dad we were together but yet in our own little worlds I wish I would have gave you more time, you and mom and everyone but I was so consumed by the pot and myself. NOW I want to give and I have nothing to give. I tried to give sonja & Tyler all the love I had and she wanted more as in material things and now she realizes how much love I was giving. It's not her fault but I want you to love her and Tammy as if they were family. I & Sonja are still praying for that second chance. If I do at some point get to make up for my bad years I want to work WITH CHILDREN Because there futures should be filled with promise and Hope. Maybe I could do some paintings and you can sell them next summer. I've got some great Idea's. I don't know what else to write now but I will write more in the morning. I think I get the phone also. I love you All!

Donald

P.S. Can I get some pictures!

PART II

The Rise and Fall of Mary Ann

Last formal portrait of the Galland family with Donald in it, 1982

6
Origins

This section of the book, which deals with my mom's addictions and crimes, is a lot harder for me to write than Part I. First, it is much fresher for everyone in my family. Second, I am much more involved personally. I wasn't even a thought when my mom and grandparents visited Don in prison and had to organize a funeral for a brother and son.

It gets harder when I have to ask my parents about events I was present at. How do I ask my dad about having angry outbreaks? How do I ask my mom about the suicide note she wrote? How do I reconcile my early happy childhood with the internal turmoil and emotional suppression both of my parents suffered from? The following is my attempt to analyze the storm, which had been building since before Don's imprisonment and death, and cataclysmically erupted during my high school years.

Also, it is important to remember that a person is more than his or her actions or circumstances. Don was more than a murderer. I am more than an alcoholic's daughter. My mom is more than her disease. Everyone is complicated and there are many reasons they are the way they are. Keep an open mind as you read and as you go about the world. Don't be quick to condemn and truly try to forgive or at least understand each other.

My mom, Mary Ann, was born on an Army base in Fort Ord, California on April 26, 1960. Her father, Robert, was stationed at the base there. When she was six months old they moved to Germany. One of her earliest memories is of tanks rolling down the street, as part of a parade or daily routine. They would also throw toy parachutes off the top floor of their apartment building. My grandma, Margaret, loved traveling and living on military bases because she met so many different people from all over the world.

In general my mom says she had a happy childhood. When they lived in Aberdeen, South Dakota, during grade school, she had many good friends. In third grade they moved to a rental house in Sioux Falls and then to a house they bought. My mom's family moved a lot because her dad was in the Army and by this time the moving had become too much. She began to feel like an outsider because she was always the new girl. Later in life her sense of being an outsider was a result of the traumatic loss of her brother and her addictions.

My mom always had a good relationship with her two older brothers, John and Louis. They supported and mentored her. Louis would encourage her to dress up for jobs. He would always ask her what she wanted to do with her life. He cemented her decision to go law school. Originally she had wanted to be a lobbyist but it is sort of impractical in South Dakota because of the limited opportunities. When she told Louis about her aspirations he said she should go to law school then. Later, when my mom was in prison, John was empathetic, especially when she was in protective solitary confinement. He made a career with the Army and had undergone solitary confinement training. Her brothers are and always have been supportive.

One tension in her childhood home was her strained relationship with her sister, Chloe. Chloe was the oldest of the siblings and often had to do more of the housework. She would think my mom was spoiled. As my mom recalls, there was some cause for Chloe to be resentful. My mom was a brat at times, partially because she was the youngest. Their brothers would often encourage the sisters fighting. Looking back my mom regrets not having a sister she was close with. She had bonded with Don, who was born when she was eight, but he passed away soon into adulthood and left my mom feeling alone.

Mary Giebink, fall 1977

My mom's relationship with my grandma was typical. My grandma was a good mom. She and my grandpa always pushed their children to succeed. They believed they could do anything they put their minds to. Both my mom and her sister, along with their brothers, have been successful in their careers and all provided lovely grandchildren, myself included.

My grandma remembers how much my mom enjoyed acting. She was a part of the community playhouse and in addition to acting was a wrestling cheerleader in high school. All along my mom worked jobs and had a strong work ethic. As my grandma remembers, my mom always wanted to be a lawyer. My grandma never knew for sure if her daughter would be successful in her goals but knew how capable and determined my mom was. Growing up she was a strong and independent girl. In other words she could be stubborn and hardheaded. Unlike Don, who was always polite to his parents, my mom was loud and argumentative.

I got to know my grandpa in his old age and I remember him as being a solely loving person in my life, but this is not how my mom experienced him. In most ways my mom's dad was a great father and husband. He was a good man, loving and supportive. However, he was raised to hit his children as a form of discipline. His own dad had belted him. Also at that time behind doors it was often considered normal or okay for men to be physically, verbally and psychologically abusive. They were the bosses and you were not to contest them.

My mom always felt that Grandpa was disapproving, that she was not good enough. Everyone told her that he was proud of her but she constantly felt the pressure to achieve. This may have influenced her overachieving mentality.

According to my mother, it was an emotional act when my grandpa would hit his children. He was in a state of rage. My grandma would cry and so would the kids. One summer, my mom was in the shower room at a camp and a girl commented that it looked like she had handprints on her butt. They were handprints from her dad. The incident was extremely embarrassing and upsetting.

As my mom grew older she began to talk back to her dad. This attribute proved useful in her later career when she had to stand up to male judges. When she was seventeen she knew it had to stop. My grandpa had been disciplining Don, who was about nine at that time, and my mom told her dad he had to stop hitting her brother. It destroys a person. Her dad threatened to take her to the juvenile detention center. In response she said go ahead, she hadn't done anything wrong. My grandpa in the end relented to my mom and the hitting of Don abated. My mom saw this anger and physical behavior again years later when she married my dad. Everyone says that women marry their fathers.

I recall my grandpa spanking me only once when I was about three. We were eating in a restaurant and I must have been misbehaving. My mom had told my grandpa he was to never hit her children. When she found out he had spanked me she was furious and he never did it again.

My grandpa got milder and more outwardly loving as he got older. When Don committed murder, some of the family went to counseling. The counselor told my mom to ask my grandpa to say that he loved her. Although he loved her, the words were never expressed. She felt that if she solicited the words 'I love you' from him, it would not mean anything. But she asked him to say it and he did. Even though she had provoked it, hearing the words come out of his mouth meant something to her. It helped. Unfortunately, she was going to need a lot more help.

Anger and aggressive behavior can result from genetics and learned behavior. It can also be a result of immaturity and for men it is quite hormonal. I am concerned these traits will end up in me, my brother, or both. Jake, my brother, and I have been known to yell from anger once in a while. We grew up in a household where our parents yelled and fought. My mom has always been a hardheaded and stubborn woman and my dad has anger issues. Their genes are ours and their behavior may become ours. In college, I play rugby. Maybe this is a safe outlet for built up and genetic aggression. Jake and I must constantly be aware of this possible genetic and learned attribute as we become adults and when we have spouses and children.

A person and his or her actions have many causes and origins. To understand my mom and her behavior it is imperative to learn about her childhood and the events that have shaped her. Similarly, to know who I am, I need to know who my mom is and how her life has affected me.

7
Round One

My mom always dated alcoholics. She was an enabler and codependent. For the majority of her life, she was the responsible one in the group of alcoholics and alcohol abusers but it wouldn't always last. When she would go to the bar she would have a few drinks and go home because she had to be up for work in the morning. My grandma always knew she smoked and drank but never said anything. She didn't know what to say or didn't want to be a meddling mother. If my grandparents had meddled, my mom probably would have told them it was none of their business.

The first time her drinking became an issue, my mom was 28 and she decided to receive treatment for alcoholism. It was an outpatient program, which resulted in six months of sobriety. Although she knew she had a problem, the pain and emotions were too much to take, especially when Don committed suicide. As her career grew over the next twenty years, so did her drinking problem.

My mom attended college in Reno, Nevada, Brookings and Sioux Falls, South Dakota and graduated from the University of South Dakota in Vermillion. After college she worked for another lawyer but there was not enough business so she decided to start her own practice, which she did in 1987 with the help of her parents. Soon after, with the help of her dad, she moved the law firm to a location on Minnesota Avenue, right across from the courthouse.

Opening a business was a bold move, especially being a woman in a traditionally male dominated field. Throughout her career she continued to crack the glass ceiling. When she graduated high school, she knew she wanted to be a lawyer and headed straight on that path. Later when she looked around and saw that many of the women she graduated with had become teachers and nurses, she thought that apparently she had missed the memo. She would attend luncheons or dinner functions for lawyers and men would ask her what lawyer she was married to or which law firm she was a secretary at. Not being recognized for her hard work and the accomplishments bothered her. The sense of not being good enough for or belonging to the boys' club added stress to her already stressful job.

During her professional career, my mom was very involved in the community. She was one of the first lawyers to be active in marketing her own law firm. This included going out and meeting people. If people knew who she was, she would get more clients. She was a member in a variety of organizations such as the Lion's Club and the Chamber of Commerce, in which she was on the Small Business Council. Over the years my mom was the District Cabinet Secretary for the Lion's Club, State President and Woman of the Year for the Business and Professional Women/USA, a member of a sorority and legal fraternity and a Paul Harris Fellow of the Rotary International. In addition, she sponsored a local adult male softball team. These are only few examples of the roles my mom has played in the community.

I could write a whole book about the good work my mom did as an attorney. My mom and her parents started the WAIT program, which stands for We Are Inmates Too, with some other families and a pastor.

My mom also was a lobbyist for the Lifers group. The Lifers group was a group of men in prison who were convicted felons serving life sentences. The mission of the group was to try and overturn the death penalty totally so that no one else would die. They also purchased items for people on death row that didn't have

My Grandma, Margaret, taking a picture of my Grandpa,
Robert, at the front door of my mom's law office.

Ribbon cutting for my mom's first law office. Don is second from the left
next to my Grandma. My mom is in the middle holding the scissors.

family members to provide for them. My mom was given the honor of bringing death row inmates televisions, stationery and other comforts. This group organized the Lifers Banquet so their family members could have a meal with them. When Don was in prison, my mom's family benefitted from this program when they attended a Lifers Banquet. These experiences were personally rewarding and also helped my mom develop professionally. Before Don got in trouble, my mom looked at clients as 'them.' Afterwards it was always 'we.' This attitude comforted clients and helped her understand their plight therefore allowing for a better defense.

My mom was relatively stable until the perfect storm hit around the time I was finishing middle school and starting high school. While Don was in prison, my mom met my dad, Brad Giebink. He had grown up in Sioux Falls, as did she. Their childhood homes were about a mile and a half apart. My dad graduated with her brother John, although my dad and mom had officially never met in high school. My dad swears they passed each other in the hallway and she would stare at him.

My dad's family had money. My Grandpa Giebink was a very successful doctor, investor in real estate, and even served seven years in the South Dakota State Legislature. He passed away in 2008, almost eight years before the writing of this book, and still people from all over town and all over the state ask if I'm related to him because they recognize my last name. My dad was the youngest of seven children. Child rearing was left to his mom and she gave it her all. My dad believes he and his siblings were just too much for her. In response she had a laissez-faire attitude and provided few boundaries for her seven kids. Two of his three brothers were close to him in age and thus a major influence as he grew up. When they got into alcohol, he soon followed.

In general it was a liberal upbringing and looking back he said he could have benefitted from more boundaries. Occasionally my dad got in trouble with his friends or brothers but nothing serious. My dad believes that having money allowed him to have more freedom or more opportunity to drink. In addition, he didn't have a job early on so he developed less of a work ethic.

Although my dad was a rebellious child, in the flower power generation, he always went to school and got straight A's. He thought it was easy, if you showed up and listened. In those days, everyone went to church but my dad remembers the kids being tucked in the basement with a coloring book. The cartoon Bible stories made it hard to take the lessons seriously.

Into my dad's thirties, nothing changed much. Somehow the character of his upbringing resulted in arrested development and delayed ambition. He was a professional student, attending several universities in South Dakota. He always took the path of least resistance, which for him meant studying Earth Science. He had always thought the topic was interesting though. Throughout his undergraduate and graduate studies he felt lost as far as his purpose in life. Partying would numb the worry and restlessness.

In graduate school he had been dating a woman who had two children. The relationship fell apart and it made him think. He decided he could do what he wanted and refused to be groomed as a geological engineer, especially because he was not happy about the mining practices in the Black Hills. In addition, he was really broken-hearted over the ex-girlfriend. Rather quickly he packed up and drove to Alaska after a quick circuit through the American West.

I've always enjoyed my dad's stories from his years in Alaska. He was a true mountain man. Originally he went up to attend a gold mining conference but soon met interesting people who invited him to travel or work with them. He fought forest fires with the Alaska Natives, pulled trees from the Yukon River after the ice broke up, and he finally started living his life.

In the fall of 1991 my dad returned to Sioux Falls with every intention of returning to Alaska, sooner rather than later. Twenty-four years later he still hasn't returned. He had come home to visit friends and see his aging parents but he was soon roped into staying. My grandpa had started a company called REG Properties, which stood for Real Estate Giebink. When my dad joined there were two dozen houses and the number of properties doubled within a few years.

At this time a relative was managing the company but he fell into ill

51

health and the company fell into my dad's lap. For over a decade my dad managed the rental houses, well into my childhood. The tenants took a toll on my dad. Many renters would not pay and often trash the houses. It really burned him out and the frustration contributed to his anger issues.

My parents were both in their thirties when they started their relationship. When my dad came home from Alaska, my mom met him through his childhood friend, Todd. Todd and my dad grew up next door to each other. At this point, Todd was actually living in Colorado and would see my mom when he was back in town. The December after my dad returned to Sioux Falls, my parents officially started seeing each other.

I was soon on my way! For three days after my mom told my dad she was pregnant he didn't say a word about it. Finally, he broke his silence and said that whatever she decided to do, he would support her. For the first time my dad was forced to think of someone other than himself and my arrival helped kick him a bit out of his self-centered mentality. My mom was 34 in 1993 when I was born in Sioux Falls.

When I was about one year old my parents decided to get married before I was old enough to realize they were not married. Their lives were joined together in 1994 in a Norwegian styled church in the Black Hills. I was left in Sioux Falls with my aunt and my grandma. Two years later, in 1996, my mom gave birth to my brother Jacob.

To me, my parents seem very different. They have differing interests and personalities. So why were they attracted to each other? Many men bored my mother but not my dad. He was smart and interesting. My dad enjoyed how independent my mom was. Neither had to worry about being responsible for the other. For a long time they lived an efficient life together. There was little emotional sharing or bonding as both were numbed or self-centered. Regardless of the stunted closeness, they lived a symbiotic life together. My mom worked and cooked. My dad cleaned, took care of the kids, managed the rental houses and made art.

My dad also liked that my mom smoked pot. It was uncommon for women to be habitual marijuana users. They both also drank, although my dad had cut down from his college days and my mom was completely

My parents, Brad and Mary Ann, on their wedding day, 1994.

sober when pregnant. Later though my dad realized my mom used drugs and alcohol too much. A once good attribute turned bad.

My parents were living in a trailer home when I was born but soon moved into a house in Sioux Falls. While I was still an infant, they moved again into another house located on the edge of town that they are still living in today. I imagine soon they will downsize now that I am out of the house and my brother has moved out and begun his higher education. I feel that since he has tasted freedom and independence, chances are he will not revert back to living with our parents.

Our house on Palomino Road has been the location for so many memories, good and bad. Although our family experienced heartache and pain in that house, it will be hard to let it go. You can still see vaguely the two spots in the hallway where my dad punched holes into the drywall out of anger and frustration. The driveway has small imprints of my and my brother's hands from when it was repaved. Also at the bottom of that driveway, a friend picked me up when I couldn't stand my mom's verbal abuse and downward spiral anymore. She had chased me out of the house and down the driveway spewing hurtful words.

At the same time, my childhood house has been the setting for so many good times, even while my mom was struggling with alcoholism and depression. My brother and I loved to sit in front of the fireplace in the winter, surrounded by my family. Although we rarely sat at the dining table, we did gather around it throughout the years for family dinners at Christmas or simply to come together with family and friends to appreciate our loved ones.

Everyone loved our roof. The house is built into a hill so you can walk straight onto the roof from the back yard. We would watch fireworks and star gaze from the roof in the summer. I can't even count the number of times we went swimming at the local pool a few blocks away and the number of birthday parties, graduation parties and other celebrations we held at the clubhouse.

My dad quit drinking in 1995, when I was almost one and a half. When he was drinking he would get angry and physical with my mom. One time while drunk he grabbed the mattress and shoved her off the bed. Finally my mom said she couldn't do it anymore and he quit drinking the next day. Unfortunately he was still a dry drunk. Although he was not drinking, he still suffered from angry outbursts.

My parents often clashed horns, especially when one had been drinking. Both aggravated the situations. In retrospect my dad has said he should have been kinder and gentler with her but he still struggled to think about anyone but himself. My dad's mom half-jokingly once said that marriage was a battle to the end, and it appeared that my parents believed that. One could also say addiction is a battle to the end. Hopefully more and more my parents choose to fight the battle of addiction rather than fight each other.

Since my mom has been in recovery, my parents have been working on their relationship with some success. They are really getting to know each other. I hear about them going on a date to the movies and it makes me so happy. For years my mom was essentially comatose. She focused on work, drugs and alcohol. She didn't enjoy music or hiking or really any other activities, which they could bond over. Now she has been awakened. The other day she gave me a CD she bought that she wanted me to listen to. I was so surprised. For as long as I could remember, she had only listened to NPR and never showed any interest in music. It's like she is discovering the world all over again.

My dad also has a hard time getting out in the world. When he is in social settings he enjoys himself but it is often difficult to get him out of the house. He was raised in a country club but he's an introvert. His reticence has always frustrated my mom, who is a social butterfly, but they are working on reconciling their sometimes contradicting personalities.

During my childhood, pot and alcohol were always present. I could always smell marijuana on my mom, in the garage or in her car. I knew where she kept her stash. When I was getting older her drinking got worse. She would drink rum and Coke, even while driving. Whenever she had a big cup I knew what was in it. I recall being on vacation and taking a sip from her water bottle. It wasn't water inside.

It frustrated me. She would be late to pick me up from volleyball practice because she was too high. One time a friend and I stole her pot stash. We didn't want to smoke it. I wanted to hide it from her so she wouldn't smoke it. Maybe I blamed the pot and alcohol for my parents' fighting. These experiences created in me a strong aversion to marijuana and it holds strong.

I will never support legalizing recreational marijuana. Many say it has medical benefits and I can believe that. I don't know the science behind the drug but I know what it did to my mom and my family. It severely affected her short-term memory then, which had a direct result on my brother and me such as when she would be late picking us up from school.

There have been a few times when close friends of mine have smoked pot. They know how I feel about it and therefore try to hide it. At those times, I have chosen to worry about myself but sometimes knowing that people I care about are partaking in behavior I consider reckless is too much to handle. I get extremely upset and emotional. Those situations bring all the pain from my childhood rushing back. For people who didn't grow up with it, they don't know how harmful pot and its associated behaviors can be. I hope they learn before it is too late. I hope my story can help explain it to them.

8
The Perfect Storm

When my mom was about 47 or 48, the storm that had been brewing picked up pace. Within relatively quick succession her dad and both of my dad's parents died. In 2002, when I was ten and my brother was seven, we were at my mom's childhood home having pizza with my grandparents when my Grandpa Galland passed away. After he finished his pizza, he had gone to the bedroom to pack for a night at the hospital. He was going to have a sleep apnea test. Previously he had had knee surgery and there was an infection in his leg. I remember my grandma going to check on him and I heard "Robert" being shouted over and over from the bedroom.

Out of curiosity, I walked down the hallway and saw my grandpa on the bed and my grandma frantically trying to wake him up. He had had a heart attack, possibly as a result of the leg infection, and died at the age of 69. All I remember after that was walking around the block to get away from the house and let the fact that my grandpa had just passed away sink in.

At the same time several attorneys and even a judge, whom my mom knew well, committed suicide for their own reasons. The judge shot himself during a lunch break in the middle of a jury trial. Two siblings from our neighborhood, whom my mom saw grow up and who baby-sat my brother and me, died in a car crash in which alcohol was a factor. The constant loss of people in her life whom she cared about was hard to weather.

In addition, my mom was going through several medical issues. Menopause appeared early and she was also suffering from serious arthritis in her back. At the same time she was managing her practice, which was in the process of moving, and she was also running for office.

In 2008 and 2010, my mom ran as a Democrat for a seat in the South Dakota House of Representatives. Being a Democrat and a woman running for office in South Dakota was major task to undertake and it added extra stress on her. She ran basically because no one else was and they needed some opposition to the Republican candidate but she put great effort into her campaign. In South Dakota you can drive when you are 14, which is a policy that originated for farm families. My mom would only let me drive my cousin's old car to high school if I had her campaign magnets on the side of the car. My fellow students knew my car as the Cadillac that had "Think Giebink" emblazoned on the side.

Perhaps the last piece of the puzzle was the disintegration of her friendships. At the end my mom only associated with users. They were drinkers, and drinking, along with pot, bonded them together. The people in her life she often thought of as friends would gossip behind her back and were not supportive and loving, as real friends should be. She realized that they were not true friends and the betrayal compounded on her growing depression.

My mom was in a state of 'just getting by.' Many people, especially users, live in that plane where in the back of their heads they know they need help but they continue to live each day unhappy, abusing alcohol or drugs. It is a psychological tornado where the brain is physically affected. Drugs and alcohol adversely affect the brain's chemistry. Addiction is a real disease. Sometimes medication can help regenerate dopamine, which is damaged by the alcohol, but it is not a science that has been perfected.

At this time, in her late forties, my mom tried counseling for her depression. She attended an outpatient program at a local hospital for six to eight weeks. They prescribed her drugs to help with the depression, but my mom continued to drink while taking the medication. My mom allowed my dad to communicate with her psychiatrist. When he called, my mom was there in her office with him on speakerphone. My dad expressed concern because my mom was drinking and using prescription medicine. Inpatient treatment should have been recommended, but nothing was done. His concerns were ignored.

I also visited with a counselor at my mom's request. My mom accused me of being bipolar or depressed but in reality I was a teenager who was in an unhealthy relationship and had an alcoholic mother. Her accusations made me question myself so my dad was convinced to get me checked out. My dad took me to get evaluated and the counselor said I was a normal teenager. Then they asked if I wanted to be prescribed medication anyway. My dad got upset and asked why. Didn't they just say I was normal? This incident fortified my dad's mistrust in doctors and medication.

Towards the beginning of the storm, my mom had moved her law firm to a newly renovated historical building downtown. Before moving in both my dad and mom renovated it with several partners. The idea was a new office, a new start. The office was elegant and beautiful. My dad even displayed his art on the walls. However, in spite of the appearance of a successful business, my mom was not getting better and the counseling didn't help. She needed to hit rock bottom and we still had a few false bottoms to get through.

During this time my mom even drove three hours to Pierre, South Dakota, to discuss her problems with depression with the Bar Association, the group that monitored lawyers in the state. She even mentioned that she was suicidal. The Bar Association was inexperienced and uneducated on what to do. Instead of insisting she get help, they simply wanted her to stop practicing law and sent her back to Sioux Falls. Not taking cases left a hole in her life that she filled with more alcohol.

Shortly after she stopped taking cases, my mom moved out of my childhood home on Palomino Road. I didn't fully understand then, but it was simple why she moved out. We wanted her to stop drinking and she didn't want to. The floodgates opened when she moved into a house only a several miles away because she no longer had anyone supervising her.

In May of 2009, she had her first DWI, driving while intoxicated. It had been raining one night and as she was driving home she hydroplaned into an electrical box. In the car was our boxer dog, Addy. My mom had bought her as a way of luring my brother and me to her house. The car accident shook the dog but both Addy and my mom were safe. My mom only had to pay a fine as punishment for the DWI so she hardly had to face the seriousness of the incident. To me, it was just another time my mom showed irresponsibility.

It was the summer after my freshman year of high school. My parents' relationship was deteriorating. My mom went on binges frequently. I was working as a secretary at her law firm. Business was slow and she was often absent. I was really inside myself that summer. I had almost given up hope of having a healthy mother and happy, complete family. It is important to remember I was a fifteen-year-old girl, hormones and all.

There was a boy named Zach. We met in orchestra class and dated for a while. He was a senior and I was a freshman. Zach wasn't your typical violin player. I knew he was a 'bad boy' and a bad influence but maybe I was looking for a distraction. We spent a lot of time at my mom's house because she let me do whatever I wanted. Most of my time that summer was spent with Zach.

Young love caught a strong hold on me and at times I turned my back on my family. However, my mom's behavior still created in me a strong aversion to drugs and alcohol so I never felt the desire to experiment. Although I now believe it was not a good idea to associate with Zach, he was there for me that summer when I needed a friend. He was there when my mom tried to kill herself.

9
The Note

I must have known it was coming. I sensed something was wrong that day. As I mentioned, I was working as my mom's secretary and that day she needed to sign some paychecks. At 10 in the morning I called her and she said she would be in by noon. After lunch she still had not showed so I drove to her house. Smiling, she answered the door in her robe and said she would be in soon. Deceived, I turned around and headed back to the office.

At closing time she still hadn't showed so I decided to visit her again. After banging on the door and getting no response, I entered the house angry and annoyed. I quickly found her locked in the bathroom in the master bedroom. "Mom, why didn't you come to the office? What's going on? Are you okay? Can you come out please?" All I got was deflection and vagueness. After ten minutes I wrote it off to her being stubborn and irresponsible and left.

It was Friday and that meant bowling. That summer my family had signed up for a parent-child league. My dad and Jake were a team. They ended up winning the whole league! I was supposed to be paired with my mom but often had to find someone to take her place. Sometimes Zach would bowl, which was the case that night.

I'd let the fun of bowling with family and friends distract me for a couple hours, but as I was driving home with my dad I remembered my mom. I had a weird feeling. Although I was tired, from the day and of her, I wanted to stop and check on her. It was hard to convince my dad to take the detour.

The last thing he wanted to do was waste more energy and time on her. At this point he had already given so much. And he would give even more in the future. A couple years before that night, he had started weekly Bible studies with a local church. It softened his mind. It wasn't necessarily religion that affected him but really considering the potential of compassion. By the time my mom was really bad, he was deeply in faith. It sustained him and without it he would have not only abandoned her but it would have been a bitter departure. In addition, my dad had extricated himself from managing the rental houses for REG Properties a few years before. It removed a major stress from his life and he was then able to focus on being a stay-at-home dad and artist.

The absence of a stressor and the addition of faith help explain why he agreed at last to stop by her house that night. We let ourselves in and soon discovered she was still in the bathroom. It had been five hours. None of it made sense. I quickly got to work. She could never hide anything from me. There were bottles of liquor in the cabinets, casino receipts in her purse, weed in her car and empty pill bottles in the bedroom.

Concerned, we threatened to call 911. Earlier that day she had filled her prescriptions. We told her that if she opened the door and showed us the pills, we wouldn't call the cops. She insisted she hadn't taken all the anti-depressants but we wanted proof. She was angry and upset with us. After a while of no progress we resigned to not calling 911. She was talking and that was a good sign. My dad and I stood in the kitchen waiting for Zach and my brother to arrive. We had called them to come to her house.

As we waited I was leaning on a drawer. For some reason I had an idea to check what was inside. There were mostly pens and junk inside but at the back was a piece of paper folded up. It was a list of people she wanted at her funeral. Now we knew why she was so angry—we had interrupted her suicide. Immediately we called 911. I asked her later why the note was so hidden in that drawer. She hadn't wanted us to find it until after she was gone.

When the ambulance came, the sheriff said, "We're taking down the door" and EMTs took the door off its hinges. It turned out that she had tried to overdose on anti-depressants but she also took a bottle of Ibuprofen, which made her throw up the pills. She had trouble opening the door and coming out of the bathroom because hours earlier she had slipped and fallen. The cocktail of medication in her stomach also made her convulse so she had hit her head repeatedly. She was too injured, physically and emotionally, to leave the bathroom on her own.

By now everyone had arrived. We all stood in the living room as she was carried out on a gurney. She couldn't even look us in the face. I don't know what broke my heart more: seeing my mom or seeing the pain blossom on my brother's face as tears ran down his cheeks. Yet tears did not run down my face. I reacted as my mom did when Don committed murder and later killed himself. I was stoic as I wrapped my arms around Jake. I remain calm under pressure and had taken up the charge of helping a family that was crumbling at its foundation. Only when I was in bed later that night did the tears start to well up in my eyes.

The next thing my mom remembers is waking up in the hospital. They had her on twenty-four hour surveillance so there was a window from her room to the nurses' station. In the hospital bed, my mom tried several more times to take her life using a plastic knife or breaking her eyeglasses to cut her wrists.

My whole family arrived early in the morning. I took great comfort in the fact that my grandma was there in the waiting room with me. When my mom finally allowed us to visit her, my dad, my brother and I entered her room. She was crying and saying we'd be better off without her and that she wanted to die.

Jake was twelve. We only spent five minutes in that room with her before I took my brother out into the hallway. How was I supposed to deal with my grief and comfort him? It's weird remembering how little he used to be now that he is five inches taller than me. He has always been a sensitive boy. His sensitivity has actually helped him deal with difficult circumstances and create closer emotional bonds with his family and friends. It was probably healthier for him to let himself cry rather than bottle the pain away.

After the hospital brought my mom back to good physical health from her suicide attempt, she was given some options. A worker from the recovery center in Sioux Falls came and spoke with her about their facility. The difference between a treatment center and a recovery center was not explained to her. She should have gone to a treatment facility where they had doctors and counselors on staff to explain the disease and help her start retraining her mind and behavior. Instead she went to a recovery center, which is good if a recovering alcoholic needs a refresher course or more of a transition after treatment.

Of course it is easy to say that maybe if she had gone to a different facility, things would have been different. But it happened the way it happened. Alcoholics need to be willing, ready and able to recover and my mom wasn't there yet. She was able to negotiate the situation with the result of a delay in her hitting bottom.

My mom was ignorant about her disease and thought going to the recovery center, versus a treatment center, came with less of a stigma. My dad and I didn't know the difference either but the doctors at the hospital should have known better. She spent about a month at the recovery center. Although she was feeling better she wasn't treating the problem. Three weeks in the executive director even said she needed more help than they could give but nothing was done. Aftercare such as AA was promoted but it wasn't enough.

At the same time that my mom was in recovery I was going through a breakup with Zach. It was messy and emotional, as teenage breakups often are. Thankfully he moved out of town so the distance helped me get over it. Since my mom was sober she was able to be there for me. It was comforting to be able to visit her and talk about love and boys. As I was growing up we had never really bonded in that way.

Unfortunately it would take a couple more years until she was able to sustain that soberness and continue the bonding. Now she is only a phone call away. It gets annoying sometimes how often she wants to chat but I have to remind myself that it really is a blessing. Not only is she sober now but also she is interested in maintaining a relationship with me. It's a work in progress. Relationships are never finished evolving.

After treatment my mom went back to work and lived with us. She was not practicing because previously the Bar had told her that if she tried to practice, they would take her license but she was still running the office. The other lawyers in the firm only suspected she wasn't taking cases and if my dad had known he would never have supported keeping the office open. She was sober for six months until January of 2010.

Sooner than later she slipped back into bad habits because she was sick and did not yet understand the disease. Also she had accomplished all the goals she had set early in her career and she didn't make new goals, thus turning from a workaholic to solely an alcoholic. This loss of purpose contributed to her continual downfall. She stopped seeing her AA sponsor and going to meetings. She also cross-addicted to gambling, a problem she hadn't had before. With the drinking came lying and hiding. Eventually she stopped going to work. My mom fell back into her unhealthy behavior because she had not yet hit her true bottom. That was soon on its way.

Jacob Giebink, my brother

10
My Story

Looking back it is hard for me to believe that all of this happened at the same time—going through high school and becoming an adult while dealing with a family crumbling at its foundation and a mother whose life was seriously in danger. This chapter touches on my experiences as a teenager and how I perceived and dealt with this critical time.

In some ways I feel I left Jake behind. The sense of older sibling responsibility is strong. I mentioned earlier that I feel responsible for Jake the same way my mom felt responsible for Don. That summer I spent most of my time away from home because I was old enough to do so. Throughout high school I worked several jobs and was involved in many activities. I would leave home at 7 in the morning and not return until 10, which left my brother alone with my parents who were at the height of their problems.

This guilt or regret heightened when he was getting into trouble during his high school years. By that time my mom was out of the woods but the family still had to rally for Jake. Unfortunately I was in college several hours away by then so I was absent for much of it. I was determined to live my life and pursue what made me happy but I felt bad for being so far away, physically and mentally. In reality I was probably just a normal teenager and young adult finding my own way.

During my first two years of high school I also took Bible studies. At one point I was fairly committed to learning more about God and the church. Previously I was not a religious child or even a spiritual one. I was baptized Catholic but my mom raised us in a Unitarian Universalist church. I had friends there and enjoyed learning about different belief systems but the routine was not for me. Around the time I started middle school, my mom and brother attended a Lutheran Church in Brandon, South Dakota. My dad had never really attended church but at this time he started studying with Jehovah's Witnesses.

As for the years I took Bible study, it was a generally positive experience. It might have been a distraction from my home life. It might have been a sanctuary. It's hard to tell. I enjoyed learning about the Bible and their beliefs. I have always enjoyed learning. Maybe I treated Bible study as another school class.

Now I do not attend any church or study the Bible. I have faith that something exists. Something or someone compelled me to open the drawer that contained the suicide note. Right now it is difficult for me to believe in organized religion but I know it truly helps many people, as it sustained my dad for years. Maybe my perspective will change as time goes on and I will find faith.

In high school I was fortunate to meet my Latin teacher. She is the most caring and devoted educator I know. Her classroom was a sanctuary for me. I spent my lunches in there doing homework. When I entered her room I was safe. She was there if I needed to talk but she knew when I simply wanted to forget and focus on learning. My teacher even recommended Gustavus Adolphus College to me, where I will soon graduate with a bachelor's degree in History. My mom has thanked her for stepping in as a motherly figure when I needed one. My Latin teacher cared about and tried to help every student.

I never allowed my family matters to interfere with my schooling. Remembering back it feels as if I was living two lives and they rarely collided. From early on I believed that my mom's problems were never my fault. She was the one who had a disease and made bad choices. I was able to separate myself from her guilt. I had nothing to be ashamed of. My mom was sick and needed help. My denying her and her problems would have only made it worse for her and for me.

One night, later in her downward spiral, she made the news for her second DWI. I was at a graduation open house with some friends. As we stood in the driveway talking, someone brought up the lawyer who got a DWI and tried to outrun the cops. Without missing a beat I said, "Oh yeah, that's my mom." At first some giggled because it almost sounded like a joke. But they quickly realized I was serious. Uncomfortable, they changed the subject.

I told my mom this story shortly after it happened and then it slipped my mind. It hit her like a brick. She had never quite realized how her life and choices had affected her family and children. I should have felt shame and embarrassment for having a mother like her but I never did. It was my job to love and support her through a hard time, not act like she wasn't my mom. Years later, she reminded me about that night. I had completely forgotten. Hearing this made my mom realize that she shouldn't be holding on to that guilt and she finally let it go.

That night at the open house also functioned in another way. My friends learned that the stories in the news are not fiction for their entertainment. They are about real people who need society to help and support them, not mock and condemn them.

Every family has its problems. Many feel that they are alone in their struggle, especially children. It has been common for families to hide their troubles, such as addiction or depression. I want people my age to know they are not alone. We all suffer but we can all make it through. It takes perseverance and might but it's possible. Turn to faith if that is a source of strength for you. Turn to friends who are probably dealing with similar issues. Pursue individual or family counseling. Be fortified in the knowledge that my family made it through so yours can, too.

11
Rock Bottom

On May 7th of 2010, a year after the first one, my mom got her second DWI. This time it wasn't as simple as a night of drinking ending in a car crash. Financial stress had built up to a point where she could not handle it anymore. Because my mom hadn't been practicing law, the office suffered. She had brought in most of the profit. So when it was time for payroll, the office couldn't cover it. Instead of asking my dad again for more money to cover the expense, which they had, my mom embezzled $16,000 out of the clients' trust accounts, money which was for their future lawyer costs.

She is quoted in a news article saying, "I didn't want to go to my husband one more time and say we need money for the business. I was depressed. I was drinking. I was gambling…I was driving drunk…I couldn't stop and see a way out." By her behavior and later reflection it is obvious she was sick and not thinking clearly.

The embezzlement was illegal and completely unnecessary. She also took an additional $4,000 to gamble and binge with. She knew a fellow coworker had noticed her crime right away. Out of shame and hopelessness she decided to drink and binge that night. Her usual hangout was a bar on Minnesota Avenue. From there she drove, drunk, to a bar closer to home. Then she called my dad. He told her not to drive, but she thought she could make it, that it wasn't that far.

About a mile from home a cop tried to pull her over for speeding. There was a previous incident where my mom had actually outrun a cop so her sick brain decided it was a good idea to run this time. She sped up to 100 miles per hour. Right past the turn off to our house she hit an intersection, which served as a ramp and she got airborne. When she hit the ground a wheel was damaged, causing her to crash into the ditch. As the cops pulled her from the car all she could say was "I just want to die."

My mom was charged with aggravated eluding, second-offense DWI and possession of marijuana and drug paraphernalia. This was on top of the embezzlement offense that was discovered earlier in the day. In jail she was initially placed on suicide watch but was eventually placed in the holding cells.

The car chase and embezzlement were all over the news. It hit me the following day at school. In the morning I used a computer at school to look at the local news station websites. They had articles about my mom. At that time anyone could comment on the articles. To comment you didn't have to create an account but simply typed in a name. People who didn't understand or even know the whole situation said vile things. Of course what my mom did was illegal and dangerous but there was no need to kick her, or my family, when we were down.

At lunch I was so upset I had to go home. Thankfully my teachers understood. That night my best friend, McKenzey, came over. I have been friends with her essentially since birth and my mom was a maternal influence on her. McKenzey even calls her mom. We read the comment sections together. Some people commented offering prayers and hope for her recovery. Whether they knew my mom or not they knew that alcoholism and depression are real diseases that require love and support to overcome.

Unfortunately not everyone saw it that way. There were many comments about how evil and wicked my mom was. Someone even commented under her dead brother's name, Don. They used his identity to say that he was proud of her criminal behavior and other unbelievable notions. I was so emotionally fired up by the ignorance that I commented myself. I used my own name and said that I was her daughter. I tried to explain that my mom was sick and all my family can do is support her recovery. I received some encouraging feedback from those who understood.

Someone, however, used my name to comment on the article. They put words in my mouth such as my mom would be out soon and that she didn't do anything wrong, she was just having fun. The vileness expressed by members of the community was horrifying and really upsetting for a sixteen year old. McKenzey, also enraged, called the news station and told them to block the comment section for the articles. She explained how outrageous the behavior was and how irresponsible it was for the news station to allow it to happen. Thankfully, the station blocked comments for the news articles about my mom. On news articles today you have to sign up for an account to comment. People are more accountable for what they say and cannot hide behind anonymity.

After my mom appeared before a judge and pled not guilty to the charges, my dad bailed her out with $5,000. Until the sentencing in November, my mom was placed on 24/7, meaning that twice a day she was to report to the courthouse and blow into a Breathalyzer. In the morning she had to blow sometime between 6am and 9am and again in the evening she had to blow between 6pm and 9pm.

Although she was not supposed to be drinking at all, she would have a few glasses right away in the morning and it was usually out of her system by the time she had to blow. Many take this risk while on 24/7 monitoring. They can't drink enough to get drunk, so it really does nothing for them but yet they crave the bottle. She learned to drink moderately but it was dangerous to go through detox without medical help.

There was little excitement between the trial and sentencing. My mom got a job delivering newspapers for a local paper. It was a demanding and low pay job but it was something for her to do.

One night she was a few minutes late to check in and she hadn't been drinking. That night she needed to loan her car to a friend who was also delivering papers. She told the officials at the Sherriff's Department that she would be right back but they thought she was making a run for it. Usually they would put a warrant out in these situations. But since my mom was a high profile case, they sent a squad of cars to surround her and bring her in. Nothing really came of the situation but the cops' reaction was overreaching.

That wasn't the case the next time. I don't remember what the rest of the day was like, but one night my mom was drunk. She had to report to 24/7 and didn't want to do so. My boyfriend, Adam, and I took up the responsibility to take her in. We drove to the courthouse around 8:30pm. My mom insisted on walking across the street to a gas station and letting her blow as close to 9pm as possible. The extra time didn't matter; she was too intoxicated. The ironic part was that the gas station where we wasted the half hour was exactly where her first law firm used to be.

Finally she let us walk her to the Sherriff's Department. As expected she blew a positive and was going to be taken to jail. I took her jewelry and wallet before they led her away. It was sad to see her so sick and helpless. All I could do was push her in the right direction and be there for her. Thankfully Adam was there for me. He has been extremely understanding and comforting these last six years.

The next day they let my mom out. Even though she had violated the program, she was released. The idea was that people like her were being forced to think about their behavior. It wasn't until prison that a real change happened.

My mom was drunk at her sentencing and drunk when she reported to the jail. She was an alcoholic. She was sentenced to eight years but all but six months were suspended because my dad had paid back the $20,000 owed to the firm. Because my mom was a lawyer, many people, including the judge, felt she should have been treated more harshly. She was supposed to be someone upholding the law, not breaking it. I disagree; no one should be treated differently under the law, even lawyers. That is the opposite of blind justice.

On the last evening of freedom, before my mom went to prison, she cooked dinner for our family and we took pictures of us for her to have while inside. We have always loved her cooking. I'm so glad I now have the opportunity to learn how to cook from her.

PART III

We Rise From the Ashes

12
Off She Goes

On November 10th, 2010 my mom reported to the jail in Sioux Falls for her prison sentence. It was the last day she drank and the first day in her journey out of the ashes. Her five-year anniversary of sobriety is coming up in November 2015.

She was held at the jail for about two weeks and then was transferred by van, in a snowstorm, to the state women's prison in Pierre, South Dakota. Her stay was to be six months with work release and probation at the end. Part 3 is composed mostly of excerpts from her journal entries, letters from her to my family and letters to her from my dad, with minor explanations by me.

No one in my family visited my mom while she was in prison. She did not want us to. One, it was winter and Pierre was a three-hour drive from Sioux Falls. Two, she didn't want us to see her in that condition. She didn't want us kids to have memories of her in a jail uniform. I never had a desire to visit her. It was my junior year of high school so I was busy with my own life. My dad was busy taking care of Jake and me, the house and the dogs. When Don was in prison my grandma visited twice a week, partially because the men's prison is in Sioux Falls, but she was mad at my mom. She was upset at my mom's behavior and often sided with my dad. Over time my grandma has forgiven my mom and is proud of her progress.

To be honest, my mom's absence didn't make much of a difference in our lives. She hadn't been around much before she went to prison. We did notice a difference in the cooking, though. My mom is a great cook who always prepared the family meals. My dad's dishes all end in 'delight' such as tuna delight or peach delight. They're delicious but he isn't an artist in the kitchen like she is. He had to really expand his horizons in the kitchen and rely heavily on TV dinners.

A TV show came out recently called *Orange is the New Black*. It centers on a white, middle-class woman who finds herself in prison, like my mom. Originally, my mom was afraid to watch it from fear it would bring back bad memories. She finally bucked up and watched it. She said it was pretty accurate. In fact, she had material for a few more episodes from her time inside. The TV show is meant to be entertaining, which it is. Often the absurdity of the situation lends itself to comedy. However, prison is not a sitcom. My mom faced serious violence and emotional disintegration. Hopefully I capture the complexity of her experience and the transformation that occurred in her.

Her mental state wavered often and dramatically. It can be confusing to read her journals, as one minute she is up and the next she is down. In prison she received treatment for her alcoholism, pot addiction and depression. Her letters were often written during times of intense raw emotion. The nastier sections, where she blames my dad irrationally, have been left out. They often talked on the phone so those conversations are lost but one can tell from the letters that at first they were very heated and unproductive.

My dad was home that winter dealing with liquidating her law firm, settling debts and trying to stay afloat financially. In addition, he was dealing with his own emotions. Overall he managed well. He provided for my brother and me, and secured a future for our family. My parents divorced around this time, mostly so that my mom could perhaps eventually file for bankruptcy and protect my dad's assets.

However, their relationship was very shaky. Both were seriously considering separating for good but in the end they resolved to work it out and be there for each other and us kids. Maybe they will get remarried someday. My grandma was a little upset that she wasn't at the first wedding. How exciting it will be if there is another chance for us all to be there to witness my parents formally recommit themselves to each other.

Communication between my parents was also difficult with her in prison. Sometimes they couldn't talk because of a mix up in the phone call credit system. Letters were slow and sometimes withheld from her. This added an extra tension on their relationship and the situation in general.

Thankfully, over time, problems were solved. My mom sobered up and started coming around to a proper way of thinking. She reflected on her past behavior and exhibits hope for the future. Inside prison she also read the Bible and attended Bible studies with Jehovah's Witnesses. It was a positive experience that fortified and comforted her.

For my dad, having my mom in prison allowed him to decompress because he knew she was safe and couldn't bring harm to the family. It allowed him to think of the situation more objectively. She hadn't acted to harm us on purpose. His anger quickly turned to compassion, which allowed him to support her through her tough times.

In prison, half of the women immediately liked my mom and the other half immediately hated her. It was partially because she was a lawyer but she also has a strong personality. At first prison did not seem that bad to her but over time the drama among the women and the inhospitable conditions wore on her. It was always unclear what the rules were so she would get in minor trouble and not know why. The guards often were either untrained to handle certain situations or outright rude.

My mom has always had a 'get work done' attitude. She wanted to fix the prison. This included making official complaints against guards who did not do their jobs. Also she complained about the poor conditions such as lack of proper clothes or filthy rooms. It is clear by the warden's response that she thought my mom was an irritant. Maybe guards were rude or seemed neglectful because it was their way of punishing her for rocking the boat.

Eventually my mom realized she needed to focus less on fixing others and focus more on fixing herself. It was safest to ignore the inmate drama and let the incompetence of some guards roll off her back.

It is important to know that she was isolated in solitary confinement twice in prison. The first time she was in protective custody but it was the same cellblock as solitary confinement. My mom had told a guard about a girl who claimed she witnessed a murder and my mom was placed in protective custody due to threats from other inmates who found out what my mom had done. The second time my mom had contracted an infection from a sliver under her nail called MRSA. She was in medical isolation to protect the other inmates from contracting the infection. Unfortunately for my mom, medical isolation meant solitary confinement. Being secluded can wreak havoc on one's mental and emotional wellbeing. From the letters and journal excerpts, it is clear that these were some of the hardest times my mom experienced.

Journal Entry 1
(Traveling from the jail in Sioux Falls to the women's prison in Pierre)
It was 5am when they woke us and told us to take all of our stuff with us. I gathered my sheets, toiletries, glasses excitedly ready for my new adventure. We walked out of the cell back to holding. Then the dreaded sack lunch for the road. Shredded turkey ham in an ice cream scoop shape plopped on a soggy piece of bread, an orange, a tasteless strawberry cookie, and a small carton of milk. When you're hungry it looks pretty good. Many times I recall passing up an orange in my prior years. Now it feels like a Christmas present to get fresh fruit.

We are able to change back into our own street clothes for the ride. Finally the bus driver arrived. Chains went around our wrists, handcuffs for our ankles, and off we go. One by one we all followed each other outside. The temperature was about 20 degrees and many of us had no coat. A few complained about the cold but I thought the air was refreshing.

In Pierre we stopped at the county jail and dropped off a young man and woman. Around the corner and we are home. By this time all of us are doing the urine dance and the pee tests are performed. Completely naked we are asked to squat and cough to make sure there is no contraband hidden. I am given socks, shirts, two towels, underwear, bras, plastic slippers, and an orange top and pants.

The warden tried to warn me that all of the inmates would want to talk to me to get advice or ask questions about their cases. After a brief medical exam I was taken to C-block.

Journal Entry 2
24 November 2010 Day One
As I came through the locked door I felt a little dazed. They took me to my new residence D-22. My roommates Ruth and Brandy were there and I put my stuff away. They told me what to expect and generously shared their commissary items. Slowly I got to know the women's names. At least two previous clients were in the unit with me. The guard did let me go to the library so I could get a book and before I knew it, count at 9:30 and to bed by 10:30.

13
Settling In

Journal Entry 3
25 November 2010 Day Two-Thanksgiving
Today we get a mixed bag of snacks. Real turkey instead of deli-sliced, what a treat! The rest of the day was ruined due to my mental state. I went to lunch and did not enjoy it. I stayed in my room crying the rest of the day. Most of the other women tried to console me.

Ca. mid November 2010
Dear Brad,

My inmate # is 54781 and to put money on my phone account you have to call 1-800-849-6081. That's why I haven't called; I haven't been able to have phone privileges. I did ask for a special call for Jacob's birthday but I don't know if it will be granted. They have taken money out of my commissary for my shoes, toiletries, and cost of housing. Evidently I cannot buy phone cards, this is the only way we can talk on the phone.

I think my release date is May 18 at 7:30am in Pierre. I may get a job or get to transfer to Sioux Falls and have work release. I'm trying to do whatever I can. My experience hasn't been too bad, except for the medical care at the jail. But overall things are going as well as they could. Of course I miss you and the kids, a lot. But I want to assure you all that I am fine and hopefully the time will go fast. Thanks for being such a great support to me. I will never be able to tell you how much you and the kids mean to me. They are amazing. I am so glad that you are so solid and loving. I hope the newspaper article in the paper was not a further distress in their already chaotic existence. The more ok we are, the easier it will be for them. I would prefer that you not visit. It is a long way and I don't want the kids to have the memories. Thanks for trying to see me last Tuesday, just knowing that you tried made me feel very loved! I am flooded with all kinds of emotions.

Could you send some family pictures? Alexa and Jacob school pictures from my wallet would be nice, also. I guess I have a lot of making up to do when I get out. I hope you will let me. But I still will not be upset or surprised if you choose other options.

I love you very much.

Thanks for all that you do.

Mary Ann

Jacob and Alexa,

I miss you guys vey much. I hope this experience is a growing time for all of us. I wish I could insulate you from all the trouble it must make for you. The one thing I know is that one lesson that can be learned is that everyone will experience highs and lows in their lives. And in order to survive one has to be able to handle the good and the bad. But I wish I wasn't the one that brought adversity to your lives. Everyone makes it sound like jail or prison is so horrible-it isn't that bad except that I can't be with you. I am safe, well fed and trying to look at the positive every day. For example, this is a new beginning and a way to start over. I hope you will open your hearts to give me the chance to start over with our relationship. The only thing I can do at this stage is to try to get better each day.

Jake, I hope your birthday was great! Alexa and Jake, Happy Thanksgiving-I am so thankful for both of you-the best part of my life is you guys!

Love, Your Mom

26 November 2010

Dear Brad,

I hope your Thanksgiving went better after our phone call. My day was pretty miserable, but holidays have never been great for us. I find it incredible that you don't think I am contrite. Do you really think I want to be here or that I wanted to hurt everyone? Of course I am sorry and I have said so many times. I am not sure that you are able to forgive me. And we will not be able to start over if you cannot. Further you need to forgive yourself for whatever you are angry about, enabling me, etc. I know that all the responsibility for everything is on your shoulders. When I try to discuss things with you it's to help, not that I am directing you to do my bidding.

I think maybe I should not come home after I am released otherwise we may just go back to our same old routine. And that hasn't worked very well. Nevertheless that's something I will figure out down the line. Until then let's just try to communicate for the kids and put the anger aside. Will not continue any phone calls if the yelling occurs. In fact I am not sure we should talk on the phone. If you could put some money on my phone account at least I could talk to Jake, Lexi and Mom.

I find it hard to believe that you can be upset about my comments that I retired and don't have to work. I have almost always worked during our marriage. Is that the pot calling the kettle black? I have given you everything; at least half of our assets can go directly to the kids.

Love, Mary Ann

27 November 2010

Brad,

It's Saturday morning, and everyone sleeps in, they have breakfast at 5am. It is a nice time when no one is around. There are 40 women and lots of drama. I suppose I should start to write that book. I still can't decide what to write about but I figure if I start maybe something will come to me. One idea I had was The Shark in the Fish Tank or The Lawyer in Prison. The fish tank is what they call the room that new prisoners are placed in when they start their sentence. The stories of the women are very interesting. Every day I feel so fortunate that my life has been so free of the kinds of trouble and heartache that many have experienced. And even if I leave here with nothing to go home to, my life is so much better than 99% of the women in this facility.

Mary Ann

Journal Entry 4

28 November 2010 Day Five

Since there is not much to do, like they won't let you have Bible study, rec, go to church, a bunch of us decided to have our own church service. I sent a message to the Chaplain that I would like a Jehovah's Witness Bible.

28 November 2010

Brad,

Yesterday I started to try and write a journal. I will probably send you the pages to keep as I write them. The gals here are really decent. Once in a while there is a little drama but it is nothing compared to the TLC drama, Recovery Center. I still have not read the article about me from the Argus although I think everyone else did. I have been trying to eat less and walk; hopefully I will lose some weight while I am incarcerated.

So I have been learning a lot of card games and found some formidable opponents in Scrabble. We are also on our 2nd puzzle. This morning we are going to have a makeshift church service. And I think I am going to be allowed Bible Study with a Jehovah's Witness from Pierre. We don't watch much TV, as soon as you start watching something the prison has count so you have to turn it off and go to your room. And even though I read 3 books in county, I haven't read any here. I figure my spare time will be spent writing.

The air is very dry and my top lip split a little, but everyone is good about letting you use their lotion, carmex, coffee, etc. We don't get our commissary until next week. They make you buy everything. You can get a TV for 140 dollars but then you just waste your time. I asked for a job (25 cents an hour).

"Shall We Dance" is on TV right now. Please call mom and let her know things are good for me. I don't have any envelopes or stamps so I can't write her yet. Maybe we should take a ballroom dancing class together. I would love that. I bet she could help us find a good class that isn't costly. Or maybe Leo and she could show us how!

The envelope can only take 7 pages so I wanted to make sure I filled it up. My roommate gave me an envelope and stamp to send this. I have been having a lot of dizzy spells from my high blood pressure. So they have put me on some medication. Exercising and losing weight will help a lot.

I believe this is going to be a really good experience for me and I hope for you also. Maybe it will give us a chance to start over. I remember the definition of insanity in AA. Doing the same thing and expecting different results. Many women here are in relation-ships with drug users and alcoholics, abusive and controlling men. They stress about going home-mostly because they don't have a lot of other options. Well I hope that you write but don't worry, no pressure.

My roommates have been so good to me. They have been here before and give me the heads up on everything. It really helps that we get along and try to help each other. They are both from the west side of South Dakota. Ruth is from Pine Ridge Reservation and Brandwine is from Bel Fouche.

I love you all very much and thankful for all that you have done for me.

Love, Mary

Journal Entry 5
29 November 2010 Day Six
When I got up this morning and dressed my t-shirt was on backwards, my orange shirt was inside out and I had no socks on. I was a wreck. A fellow inmate looked at me and told me I needed more sleep. I agreed.

Journal Entry 6

30 November 2010 Day Seven

Today I am told that the rumor around the room is that I am a snitch. Cindy and her gang are trying to isolate me from the other gals. My friends just laugh it off.

Journal Entry 7

1 December 2010 Day Eight

We got real shoes yeehah! I can already tell the difference in the way that I walk from those plastic slippers. My feet are happy. Climbing the stairs I don't feel pain in my knees.

14
How To Move Forward

1 December 2010

Hi Mary Ann,

    I really liked nearly all of what you said in your letters. The problem is that in the past your actions have not matched your words. I realize you have 'issues' and that you have made efforts to deal with some of them. What I really need is for you to truly confide in me and not to internalize everything. That is how you get close to people. That is how you build trust. I need to be able to trust you. You also, in my mind, need to get a handle on the value of money and understand that we have little security and are barely scraping by. Yes, I have anger and I have difficulty forgiving but a lot of that, I believe, comes from the frustration of not being able to trust you and in all the problems, which result from this condition.

    I have talked to a car dealership about selling the CTS but that may be a while as Alexa had trouble with the Trooper during a recent blizzard. I now don't think Alexa is comfortable with the Trooper and she doesn't want to drive the Subaru. She will have to pick between the blue car and the Trooper if I am to sell the CTS.

    I am sorry about my behavior during our phone conversation. I didn't mean for it to go that way. I have not been emotionally, mentally or spiritually healthy for some time now, as you should know. But I can't allow my depression to steer me into grossly detrimental acts, and nor should you allow yours to do so. It only fuels the depression. I am also sorry to hear about your physical ailments but am glad to hear you are being treated and are doing things to get in better shape. Hopefully, this time will give us both time to heal. In my mind, we have to get better for the children.

I may be angry towards you Mary Ann, but I also have a lot of compassion for you. I know this is not how you wanted our lives to go. I have said this before-I am committed to you. It would make things a whole lot easier for both us, and the children, if you allowed yourself to truly join me in matrimony and to not think of me as outside of yourself, and the same goes for me. For this we need absolute confidence and trust. Right now I can't say that I have that in you, and you apparently have not had it in me. There is still hope but we will be able to overcome the large trial ahead of us only if we fully embrace this chance to get it right. We owe it to the children, and to your mom.

Your discussions about your being sorry and about my response to your video interview don't make any sense to me. When you tell the world that you don't need to make any income it just doesn't jibe with the fact that you have built up tremendous debts not to mention the need to keep up with monthly bills and to provide for the children's secondary education. Yesterday I opened up an invoice from a jewelers that showed you purchased something in the amount of $7,392.44 on May 27, a couple of weeks after your capture. How can I think you have any sincere contrition when you indulge yourself with some overpriced trinket when you not only don't have the money to pay for it but have not done anything to try and reimburse the children for the monetary loss they incurred from your hubris?

Your actions don't match your words. As far as 'giving me every-thing' that is not saying much when you transfer over titles to cars for which I paid, and do a quick claim deed to a house that has less than zero equity. How can I give half of our assets to the kids when I am trying to ensure that bills will be paid for the next few months? I also have to consider that there are a number of judgments against you with an unknown number more coming down the pike, and that I have no idea how all that is going to play out since everything is communal property of which they can grab half. I am hoping that you will get to a point soon where you can see how irrational your thinking has been and that you will regain control and then you can start making good decisions and begin acting effectively in making amends.

At this point I feel strongly about putting everything behind us but I feel complete and lasting forgiveness can be accomplished only when I can trust that you have put behind you behavior that is so terribly detrimental to the wellbeing of every member of our family. Perhaps if we can place our trust into the wise guidance of God then that day will come.

It is Saturday so the mailperson will be here soon so I am going to wrap it up. For the sake of all that is good and holy in our lives I pray that you come out of there a renewed person who can help me to nurture and care for our children in the manner that is needed.

With all the love I can muster up, Brad

1 December 2010

Dear Brad, Alexa and Jacob,

Today has been pretty busy. I had my physical exam and requested that I be put on a special diet so I could lose some weight. It took me a week to get some shoes but now I can do some walking. The food is not too bad but they serve a lot of high sodium and carbs. I requested a job but I haven't got one yet so I have been trying to write daily just to keep the memories, maybe I will be able to put it into a book. How's mom doing? I hope you guys check on her every so often. I have received 3 letters already from people that I haven't seen in years. One couple from Brookings sent me a Thanksgiving card that was very sweet. It was nice of them to write to me.

I asked for a Jehovah's Witness Bible and have Bible studies set up with a woman from Pierre. She is a nice breath of fresh air.

93

Speaking of which I hear it has been winter since I left. You really can't tell what the weather is like because the building is made out of cement block. One evening I heard the wind whipping outside. I think it was around 50mph. Have you gotten much snow yet?

Most of the guards are pretty nice, only one or two are pretty grumpy (all the time). And the other gals are pretty decent, too. Many are to be here for longer periods than me. Well almost 2 weeks have gone by and I hope this finds you all healthy and happy. I love you all very much and miss you a lot (the dogs too).

Take care, Mom

Journal Entry 8
2 December 2010 Day Nine
Mail comes after dinner and I didn't get any but I got a job. I am so excited. I work for about three hours cleaning places that probably haven't been cleaned in a very long time. It is nice to feel productive. Who would have thought my pay would have gone from $250 an hour to 25 cents an hour.

6 December 2010
Dear Brad,

I am obtaining divorce forms and I will be filing bankruptcy for myself and for Galland Law Firm one year later. I will give you everything except a few personal items. You can have the ownership of the building and also my life insurance policy to cash in or keep active. Any leftover residuals from the assets of Galland Law Firm will go to you. When I am released I will get an efficiency to live.

I ordered the wedding ring before my 2nd DWI. I tried to call you back on Sunday to discuss this but you refused my call. I call for a little emotional support and every time I feel worse after talking to you. From now on I will be talking only to the kids and my mom. I cannot deal with your depressing phone calls. It is hard enough in here. Please just collect my mail for me until I get out. I have nowhere to keep any documents.

They have a program here for me to work and save up money for the rent and deposit. Please tell everyone that they will just have to wait to deal with me when I am released and that you have nothing to do with resolution of the debts.

I really wanted to talk to Jake Sunday and was very sad that I could not. Some of the inmates are picking on a gal in here and now are threatening to jump me when I am not looking. I was having a very hard day. Not once have you asked how am I doing. I always hope that our phone calls will help to pick me up, however I feel put down when I get off the phone.

I would rather go it on my own, penniless than continue our relationship, which is full of sorrow and disappointment. I believe my depression has increased due to the constant conflict from our situation and the only way I will be able to overcome my spiral of decline is to start clean and fresh. I may even move to Minneapolis to live with Louis if probation will allow it.

The only good thing is I have been reading the Jehovah's Witness material and that has been very uplifting.

Sincerely, Mary Ann

Please save my diary until I am released.

Journal Entry 9

6 December 2010 Day Thirteen

I get a request to go to the Sergeant's office and I am asked if I want to be put into protective custody. Some of the inmates are threatening to jump me. He believes that they may be envious, and many of them may have had bad experiences with their own attorneys. I decline. I am not afraid. I think that it is all puffery (i.e., blown out of proportion). One inmate told me don't play their game. They want to get a reaction.

Finally I call my mom, I miss talking to her every day and I feel terrible for what I have put her through these last few years. But I wasn't really in control of my life. I allowed drugs and alcohol to be in control.

It was a busy day and I cried five times. I don't think I will work tonight mopping the floors. I tell my coworkers and go to bed. Last night I slipped and fell after I finished. Thankfully I didn't get hurt too badly.

Journal Entry 10
7 December 2010 Day Fourteen
At 1:30 we have an orientation class, which I wish we should have had the first day. The information was invaluable. They went over what you can and can't do.

7 December 2010
Brad,
I hope this letter finds you well. I really liked reading your letter. If this is to work you also have many issues to work on. In your letter you talk about that we have little security. One minute you are ready to sell some of our valuables but so far have been unwilling to do so to help out with our situation.
I talked to mom last night and she needs our comfort, no doubt. Please send Jake over to see her occasionally. Maybe Alexa and Jake could sleep over on X-mas.
I don't believe you are sorry about your behavior because it never changes! You do absolutely nothing to change your depressive state and of course that has affected me and the kids. I cannot go back into that situation unless you get help also.
Mary Ann

Journal Entry 10
8 December 2010 Day Fifteen
Last night I got a letter from a court reporter for a judge. It was very uplifting. Her judge committed suicide during a jury trial. I am sure that was very difficult for her and I am sure the article about me brought back some memories. Depression is very misunderstood. The judge's death affected me. He was an excellent judge and the legal community was shocked. I remember being very sad about his death for a long time. I am sure that I had severe depression at that time. Thank God I am alive.

8 December 2010

Hello lover,

I think I am beginning to feel better about things. A lot of that has to do with you, and the way it looks like you are coming around to a better view of things, especially of me. Are you now ready to get close to me and trust me so that I may do likewise with you? Also with a few friends, whoever doesn't have drinking and/or gambling problems. Choice of association is almost everything.

I am doing fairly well with keeping the fort down, although I sure could use some help. I very much want you back to take up your part, but only if you focus on family and recovery. Of course, money is going to be a big part of the equation.

I am extremely grateful that you were not successful in total self-destruction. In truth, the last thing I ever want for myself is to repeat what I have had to take from you these last years, but if we can somehow get a better marriage out of going through this ordeal then I may come to think it was worth going through. You had initially been the giving one, trying to make the world better, but had somehow lost your way, whereas I had always been the one standing on the sidelines. Now I think it is my turn, and I have accepted as my mission bringing you home and to give what I can in nursing your wounds.

I love you, Brad

Journal Entry 11

14 December 2010 Day Twenty-One

Health Services called me in and a doctor gave me a complete exam. Her assistant had on some green antlers with red Christmas jingle bells. It made me smile.

The pen I got from commissary was blotting ink everywhere so I traded it for a pencil. Some people try to steal pens and pencils from other places like classrooms. In fact one time a red pen was missing from the library and they had a shakedown in the cells. I couldn't understand until someone said they use it to make tattoos.

15
Protective Custody

Journal Entry 12

15 December 2010 Day Twenty-Two

Yesterday a woman mentioned that when she quit meth she lived in Pipestone, Minnesota and she knew a bust was coming down because of a feeling that she had. She warned everyone that cops had been following her and she stopped cooking it in her lab. One month later everyone got busted and the snitch was killed. She did not do the killing but she watched it happen through binoculars. The person's body is at the bottom of a lake and has not been found yet. This came out while we were playing hearts, laughing and having fun. I tried to remain jovial but was shocked. First that she told us but also that it was told in such a casual and nonchalant manner.

15 December 2010

Hi Mary Ann,

I just received a letter from the prison giving me information about things. It would have been nice to receive it a couple of weeks sooner. I don't know why our phone call was dropped. All the phone company can tell me is that there are still funds available to make at least one call.

I agree that we need to stop slinging arrows at one another. The kids are doing OK. Alexa has pink eye right now for the second day. The drops don't seem to be helping too much so it must be viral. Jacob got new shoes, as big or bigger than mine. Maybe I can borrow them. He had his holiday jazz circuit yesterday where they go around to the elementary schools to play. He enjoyed it.

How are you making out? How is the rash and blood pressure? It sounds like not everyone is your friend there. For Pete's sake I wish you would pipe down a little and keep more to yourself. But that is not who you are. You are compelled to stand up for the disadvantaged. That might be your best quality, but not your safest, at least not now. Let me know when you need something and I will try to accommodate you. I am sorry for not writing more. I guess I have been too absorbed with the things around me, and to be honest, I am finding it hard to know what to say. I will do better and I will get the kids involved. We all love you and miss you and hope and pray that you are doing well.

Brad, Alexa, Jacob and the dogs

Journal Entry 13

17 December 2010 Day Twenty-Four

Almost the entire C-block has turned over in population; only nine out of 41 are inmates that were here when I came into the facility. Four of them are pregnant and want to be moved out of the fish tank. About five of us are waiting to be classified. Since today is Friday we are hoping that we will be sleeping in a different bed by tonight.

When I went to the library, I tried to get something humorous. The section had only thirty books. No wonder everyone is so depressed here. As I get older I realize more and more the value of a good laugh. Like the problem with a diet is the first three letters DIE. But I lost ten pounds, however, I don't recommend prison for a diet spa.

17 December 2010

Hi Mary Ann,

It was nice talking with you last night. The civility of our interaction has helped put me better at ease with our relationship; I hope it was the same for you. We need to build on this and avoid missteps at all costs. There is always a chance to turn things around if we work together, and to do that we need to communicate with openness, respect, and most importantly, restraint. That is, I believe, what was the stumbling stone in the course of things, not the absence of Love or passion. We are both passionate people. I think we just need to focus it on the positive.

Enclosed is an envelope with the money order, a couple of notes from your kids, and a couple of holiday cards from big politicos. Let me know if there is anything else you would like. In anticipation of our next communiqué, Brad xxo

19 December 2010

Hello lover,

Not much to report, unless you want to hear about more problems with the house, e. g. the garage door spring breaking. Awfully cold and snowy. Wish you were here to keep me warm. I guess the dogs will have to suffice.

Your mom seems to be doing a lot better. You might already know but she plans on going to Texas for a month pretty soon. Good for her. I told Alexa that in Adam she had a good combination of laid back and likes to keep busy. So she asks if that made him a keeper and I replied that I don't know him that well. Then I said that Adam might find her not laid back enough, and he piped in 'yeah.' They're cute. I'm still concerned about Jacob. His bubbliness seems to be morphing into teenage malaise. I did get him signed up for driver's education in early summer.

The dogs are not getting enough exercise, kind of difficult to run them outside with the deep snow and cold. I hope you are still making progress toward health and wellbeing. I believe you when you say that nobody could have gotten through to you to tell you

101

that you were not living a dimensionally full life. I tried, probably in a poor way; I was not in my right mind either. Not as bad as you of course, you were way gone. We just can't be like that anymore. Have you done a Bible study yet? Now I am just jabbering so I will close with 'I love you, I miss you and I need you. ' To qualify the last part of that statement I need to add 'but only if you feel the same and will do whatever it takes to keep from going back to the dark side.'

   Your man, Brad

Journal Entry 14
24 December 2010 Day Thirty-One, Christmas Eve
I haven't written in the last few days because of a series of incidences. As I wrote earlier, a woman told me about a murder she witnessed five years ago in Minnesota. After a few days and much thought I felt it my obligation to the relatives of the individual to tell the authorities. At first I tried to tell an officer on December 17 while I was mopping. She ignored me. The next day I told another officer. She immediately sent me to the sergeant's office where I told him the story. That day I slipped and fell going through the chow line. After eating I went to Health Services to get a card for Tylenol and they gave me a medical order that said I was allowed ice in a zip lock bag to put on my sore spots. December 19th I was refused by an officer and a sergeant ice for my injuries. December 22nd I filled out a grievance form against the officers for disobeying the medical order.

   After I wrote the grievance, I was sitting with the alleged murder witness when the assistant warden pulled her away from her dinner. When I returned to C-block shortly thereafter, the alleged murder witness was in the complete opposite corner of the room. She lifted her hand pointing her finger red in the face and yelled, "Don't you ever fucking talk to me again." I went to my room. A few moments later another woman came to my door, which is against the rules, put her face against our window and shouted "You're fucked!" I immediately called the officer in the control booth for help and said, "I am afraid." Immediately three officers came into my room. I explained the situation. After count and lockdown they unlocked my door and I went to the sergeant's office. I explained the situation again and they put me in temporary protective custody. That's when the nightmare began. I was told to strip and was given a sleeveless tunic. I was placed in a cell with a camera and only a pillow and blanket. It was only supposed to be 48 hours but it has now been 50 hours and I am still here. The walls and ceilings are spotted with food, wet toilet paper globs, and maxi pad adhesive. I was not allowed to clean the room until this morning although I couldn't clean the walls with what they gave me. Even the guard said it was disgusting. The assistant warden had come to the block for inspection on December 23rd. I asked him to look at the room and he refused, and then told him about my back problem. They had me sleeping on a metal slab with a very thin pad. He said I could talk to medical services.

Every guard treats me as if I am on disciplinary hold. In fact, they wanted to handcuff me to take me to the shower and I stated that I am in protective custody and should not be handcuffed. That changed their minds. My next-door neighbor has been in her room for eight years and has three to go. I am slowly talking to her so that she can have some human contact. I think the guards forget she is human.

They won't let me have my Bible. When I keep asking why are you punishing me the only response is, "We are not, we always do this for 48-hour holds." If I was a suicide risk or disciplinary problem I could understand such treatment. I believe the inmates are less of a risk to be around than the guards in the block. Every guard that was kind to me in C-block becomes mean and uncaring when they step into A-block, solitary confinement.

This morning I cried because finally a guard was concerned for me and hunted for my lost shoes, and last night another guard was so nice in tracking down my personal items. I can't tell you how nice it was to read my husband's letters, call him on the phone, and see my children's faces in the pictures he sent. I even got a holiday card from Obama. Since I have been here two friends have died and I have had to miss their funerals. I hope their families are okay this time of year.

24 December 2010

Dear Brad,

I miss your kisses. You know you were right in your first letter that this is not the way I planned our lives to go. But I think this may be a positive experience for me. It is like starting over and I sure appreciate the small things. Like waking up and falling asleep to your and the kids' pictures, the value of a cup of tea or coffee, the smell of perfume and the attention of our dogs. The precious time I have left with mom or the few minutes I get to see my brothers or sister.

But most of all your forgiving love and kindness. You are the best (okay, some days not the best.) I have cried a lot the last four days and I wonder if I am just feeling sorry for myself or if I am really growing. I know the Jehovah's Witness material is really helping me make it through this tough time. I hope you keep up the Bible studies. Christmas is a special time of year. Every day is, no matter where we are, but I am ready for your dreams now. Mine did not work out so well. Alaska?

Love, Mary

Jacob,

Well I just talked to you on the phone. It is always such a bright spot in my day to hear your voice. I couldn't be prouder of what a young man you have become and a good snowboarder, sax player, student, girl chaser (just kidding), son, bowler, where do I stop? I have been reading funny stories to keep my spirits up while I miss being home with you all. This is a good chance for me to realize what a great family and life I have; thank goodness I can have a fresh new start on life.

Tonight we get goodie bags of taco chips, pretzels, cheese puffs, cookies, rice crispy bars, chocolate (all the things you like) and olives, sweet pickled peppers, carrot sticks and celery (all the thing I like) along with ranch dressing, salsa and cheese dip. If you are going to be here I guess this is the day because you don't get treats any other time. Remember there is always a positive to everything. Louis said he sent you a gift and some money so you can buy something for yourself.

Are you practicing driving? In the snow is a good time to learn! Especially when I'm gone! I have been busy trying to lose weight (lost 10 lbs.) and working for 25 cents an hour. Maybe if I write a book I can make a little cash for our trip to Alaska, do you still want to go?

Please hug and kiss Alexa, Grandma, your Dad and the dogs too (oh, did I forget Adam-you don't have to kiss him, just a big hug). Can you believe those two have been together 1 year, wow.

I love and miss you, Mom

25 December 2010

Dear Alexa, Jacob, Brad, Mom

Well I think tomorrow or Friday they are moving me out of the fish tank into another room that is minimum security and I will be able to go outside. Then I will have a lot more freedom and I will finally be able to attend Bible study, recreation, Christmas programs, AA and lots more. Tomorrow is also when I get my holiday gifts. Thanks for providing them for me.

I have met some nice people from all over the state. My roommate is a young Native American girl named Angel who has 2 kids. She talks about going to college and maybe joining the army someday. I couldn't have a nicer cellee as we call our roommates.

I just got a new pair of glasses. They don't give you much of a selection and the frames are pink. They remind me of frames that I wore in the 80's. The chemical dependency and mental health want me to do 5 or 10 weeks of treatment. Either way I plan on getting as much as I can out of these programs so I can come back and be a good wife, mother and daughter.

I love you all very much and miss you very much. You continue to

*make me very proud to be in your lives. I hope someday I can get
back your respect and trust.*
   All my love, Mom

Journal Entry 15
26 December 2010 Day Thirty-Three
Things are better now. The toilet didn't flush in my room so they
moved me. I get two hours a day in the day room so I can walk and
make calls. I am so lucky for my mother and brothers for making
my kids' Christmas a merry one.

Journal Entry 16
29 December 2010 Day Thirty-Six
I started working on some depression material and realize that I
have done a lot of the right things to help keep the depression
at bay but drinking sure wasn't one of them. Drinking and
smoking were the opposite of what I need to turn the
depression around.

   I think 8 years in here is a big hammer over my head to help to
me to resist those old temptations. But I still have that lingering
thought of that old glamorous life. What foolish thoughts. Nothing
about it was glamorous. The sneaking and lying and secrets to
have to keep. The waste of time looking for it, getting it, hiding
it, using it and then hiding the fact that you got drunk or high and
really never enjoying it or your life or existence in general. What a
waste of energy and time.

Journal Entry 17
30 December 2010 Day Thirty-Seven
Well it's 9 on Thursday and the inspection is about to occur. I don't
know why they don't go into any of the rooms in the hole. They are
so concerned with the appearance but don't look where the real
filth is, in A-block.

   When I first came here I really didn't think there were a lot of
fights but as the days go by and the women just keep coming. I see

I was mistaken. Especially yesterday when the gal had her face split open and was bleeding.

30 December 2010
Hello wife,

Sorry, but I am not much in a writing mood and I want to get your money order into the mail so this is going to be short. I am very glad to hear that your living conditions have improved. I just talked with your mom and she said that her cell phone went dead when you were talking with her. She said that you two had a nice talk until it went dead.

In your letter you said that maybe it was time to pursue my dreams and you wrote the word 'Alaska'? Maybe some day it would be nice to go there and explore possibilities. Right now, however, I just want to see us both healthy and productive and more engaged with the wellbeing of our children. That is now my dream and I hope yours too. You and I have been too self-involved, and we let our poor relationship hurt our innocent children. Let's help them develop some worthy dreams and then help them pursue those dreams. They are growing up so fast and soon we will not have much of a chance to make amends to them if we don't start now and do a good job.

One thing this separation has given us is time and room to breathe and reflect. I can't help but feel like I still don't know what is at the root of what has gone so wrong. We both have addictions and we both have depression but that has been true, at least for me, all of my adult life. So what caused the wheels to come flying off these last few years? Whatever it is, I think I know what will help us to overcome it. We need to start acting like a team, and that involves confiding and trusting. You are right, we need a new start. For that we need to be new people. The only way I see that this is possible is if we embrace spirituality, God, whatever you want to call it. I have been amazed and enthralled at the transformation of a number of people close to me over the past ten years and have felt the potential myself.

People who exhibit real faith, whether it be Catholic, Protestant or Witness, speak of love and forgiveness and security.

107

These people were all much like us and they usually found their spirituality while going through difficult times. I have to believe that the same can happen for us, for if I don't hold that belief, then I think I will lose all semblance of hope for us. I am glad you are reading the JW magazines. It seems to me that the beginning of the path starts with taking in information, otherwise we do not know where or how to step. Another critical thing for us right now is to remain up building because it is much easier to tear down a framework than it is to construct. And we have become quite expert demolitionists in our marriage. It is time for a real change. It is time to throw away our pride and become truly humble. It is time to more fully recognize the good gifts we have been given.

I told you, Mary Ann, that I need you, and I would like to think that is true of you also. Of course, the person we each need has to be the nice one within us. Even though the children need for us to be good parents, it is essential that we do it for each other first and the rest will follow.

With peace and love, Your Hubby

---

31 December 2010
Brad,

I requested no sugar in my cereal or coffee but of course both had sugar. No heart healthy diet for those in A-block. I have requested another grievance form. 1) for violating my medical order of a heart healthy diet 2) not allowing commissary. Vickie told me to get commissary for the hypoglycemic periods at night since I have been borderline diabetic. I heard about a time when there was an inmate council that would meet with the guards once in a while to work out concerns. It sounds like a good idea.

Mary Ann

1 January 2011
Brad,

I had a nice long walk and talk today. I'm beginning to think all of this is a kind of retaliation for the grievance I filed on December

21st. At 3pm I asked for a new pencil, we have to exchange them in order to get one that has been sharpened. I had eaten supper and fell asleep to wake to Charity and Ashley and another inmate screaming 'you fucking bitch' at each other. I realized it was 5:50pm and I hadn't got my pencil. I called the control booth and they said I need to ask the guard as they walk by, the shift changed. They all refused me.

Finally the Sergeant came into the block because 2 more inmates were brought in after a fight. One went to 48-hour hold. I luckily got the Sergeant's attention and told him that I had been refused a pencil. Five hours after requested, I finally got a pencil.

The pictures are great! I love you, Mary

Journal Entry 18

4 January 2011 Day Forty-Three

I got classified! The more I am in this room in the hole the more writing I discover on the walls, bed frames and doors from all the women in before me. I wonder why they write their names when they could be written up for it. I bet they felt like I feel. What more could they do-take away my birthday. I have been in isolation for 14 days now and in prison for 46 days. Oh man, my hair is getting long and I need a haircut desperately. I love looking at my new pictures of our dog, Addy, in my chair waiting for me. Lexi and Jacob on the last night before I came in and my mom smiling happily.

4 January 2011

Hello lover,

Went bowling with the kids and Adam last night. Lot of fun, I killed them. Alexa beat Jacob's two-game total by two pins. In two games I got THIRTEEN strikes and six spares. I still got it. Alexa and Adam want to make these outings a tradition. Sure would like to have you with us. I think you would be very competitive with the other three.

Enclosed are the lyrics you wanted. Let me know what other songs you would like. Can't you get a radio there?

Talked with a lawyer last night. He didn't find any credence to the girl's story in Minnesota. If the girl was lying then maybe you are not in as much danger. The lawyer tells me the warden thinks you need to stay put for the duration of your sentence and to go through alcohol and drug treatment. So he doesn't think a hearing will be successful in getting you moved. For me, it is hard to know the truth and what is right and what is best. I feel for your predicament and so does the lawyer, but prison is not a good place under any circumstances and you may have to just bear with it. I think you need to protect yourself by not interjecting into other people's situations.

Now that you have had some time to clean out your system and to think about why you are there, I hope you have a better idea of how out of control you have been for the last couple of years, and how helpless the kids, your mom and I have felt. In order for you to truly learn from your missteps and to avoid repeating them when you get out I think it is very important that you come to terms with precisely what all it is that you have done. I am trying to do the same because I know how badly I have handled my end of things. Too often I was more worried about money, about what you were doing, than about you. I admit it, I confess, I was wasting too much effort trying to get into your head when I should have been trying to get into your heart. For had I done that, the other becomes unnecessary. My bad. I am so very sorry.

Do you realize that if we were to marry our fine qualities and individual strength together that the product would be a glorious union? The sum of you and I would be so much less than us. I suspect that my writing is wordy, and directed primarily toward my own reasoning. Again, my bad. I want to be reaching you. Am I? Open, and honest, and courteous communication is key to any winning game plan.

I just got off the phone with you and I share your indignation and frustration with how you are being treated. I can only imagine what it is like for you. I will try to do what I can to help ease your

110

suffering. Stay hopeful and keep aware so that you may survive to enjoy much better days.

*   With heartfelt love, Brad*

Journal Entry 19
5 January 2011 Day Forty-Four
I just talked to the lieutenant asking to be removed from protective custody. He said yes. He instructed the guard to give me a note and take it to him directly. I can't quit crying. Too many times have I had my hopes up only to be dashed.

Journal Entry 20
6 January 2011 Day Forty-Five
I am still in shock that I am out of A-block.

16
Seeing the Light

Journal Entry 21
7 January 2011 Day Forty-Six
I need a job. I am so bored and feel like I am just going to get into trouble if I don't have something to do. I think that is probably true on the outside.

7 January 2011
Dear Brad,
  I loved your letter yesterday. You were funny introspective and even poetic. I really love writing to each other. It is like seeing another side of each other that has been hidden for a while. I still can't get a handle on how long I may be here. I don't know when treatment will start or how long it will be. I'm just trying to keep my nose clean. Valerie and I are sitting out in the day room writing in our journals.
  Did Jake take the quiz on addiction to video games? I can't believe how well you bowled and thought it was cute you said I might be competition to the kids. And maybe a little egotistical, I will try to be competition to you. What a great idea for a family tradition.
  I can't believe the gamut of emotions that I have had. Take away

mind-altering substances and I always heard that would be true but to go through it I feel like I am starting over as a teenager. They talk about how we stop maturing at the age we start drinking, or drugging and I am sure that is true with me. I have so much maturing to do. You certainly could not have told me that before.

Being in A-block helps one to separate priorities and minor annoyances. Like last night I was in the bathroom when they called Rec. I hurried and the control room guard would not let me through the gate. He was really quite rude and unfair. But I realized maybe I will get ready a little earlier and be ready to go before 8:30pm.

Thanks for the phone money. I would not be able to make it through this without all your support, love and unconditional understanding. There is nowhere to go but up.

All my love, Mary Ann

Journal Entry 22

8 January 2011 Day Forty-Seven

Linda heard me talking in the shower. We have become friends and she lets me read her newspaper. There are 96 women in a very small area and only curtains for doors. Lots of stories and lots of work to do. I start Monday in the laundry, thank goodness. It's good to have a job.

Well I just got back from Catholic Mass. At first I went because I am so bored and it was something to do. What a great experience it was. I'm not sure I can even put it into words. The emotions were so overpowering. I grew up Catholic and have been pretty angry with the institution for many years. I have closed myself off from the Catholics. But I start to well up with tears when I remember how important the church was in my life. In fact, at one point I wanted to be a nun or missionary. I sat next to 2 inmates who were here because they killed children. I had this overwhelming feeling that if they could move on and live life then maybe so could I. I keep thinking what a terrible person I am; yet there are also lots of good things about me I tend to downplay. I always just want to forget my stupid or criminal behavior and if I don't think about it maybe I

114

don't have to face up to it. But in Mass it was all there. And the best part is that even though we all sin (on different levels) we all can be forgiven, mostly by ourselves.

I told Brad the best part of all of this is the unconditional love I feel from him, the kids, my brothers, and some of my friends. Mostly with Brad. I cannot say I would have been so steadfast as he has been.

Journal Entry 23
9 January 2011 Day Forty-Eight

I can't wait until tomorrow. Today I reflected back on my suicide attempt and had a very tearful time. I can't believe what I put my kids through but of course I wasn't able to be concerned for them. In fact, I thought they would be better off without me. I really need to take this time to reflect and think about how I can protect myself from going down into that depression tornado. I hope I can recognize the signs and get help or assistance when these things are bound to happen again.

Journal Excerpt 24
10 January 2011 Day Forty-Nine

Today was my first day of work in the laundry. I am so glad to have a job. In a lot of ways it feels as if I'm starting all over again. Physically I am so out of shape and have so many problems. One gains a lot of respect for the laundry workers working there.

Journal Excerpt 25
15 January 2011 Day Fifty-Four

Well I have found my anti-drug in cards. We played last night and laughed until our sides hurt. It didn't matter if we won or lost because we had so much fun. Linda told us about her 50th birthday when she had her nose pierced. I don't understand why anyone wants a body piercing. She said she was pretty intoxicated and high so she didn't feel much pain. Linda and I have a lot in common. Her husband committed suicide about the same time my brother did. Our age and changes are about the same and her son said when he read the article about me, he thought of her. It helps to know that there is someone out there that is like you so you do not feel isolated and insecure. However, many times the stories of past escapades are glorified. I just think that's what got us here, what fun was it really. We were self-medicating because we were so unhappy inside.

16 January 2011
Dear Alexa, Jacob and Brad,

Slowly I start to see the past in a new light. I cringe at the memory of my suicide attempt and the haunting memory you must have from it. I will never forget how distraught I was in the hospital when I said that you would be better off without me. In fact, I thought about how you don't have me around right now and you seem to be doing well. But I can't imagine the pain a child must feel to have a parent commit suicide and have to live with that pain. Besides I have years of making up to do to repay you for the money I took from you.

This experience gives me time to reflect on all the crazy thinking I had. Drinking was more important than anything else. I really regret the school activities you were in that I didn't attend. And I thank God that your dad and grandmother were there to pick up my slack. I hope I can live a life that will allow you to trust me again. And more than anything I hope it's not too late. I know that you are at the age when your friends are sometimes more important but I hope you will give me a little of your time to do things together.

I have been working full time in the laundry and work is physically demanding. I like it and I think it will help to get me in better shape. This morning I mopped the floor while everyone was sleeping (98 women). My roommate was telling me I was snoring last night; I suppose you don't miss that noise.

I hear Brad is trying out new recipes. How is his potato salad? I can't wait to have you guys make me my first real meal when I get out. Everyone wants either steak or pizza. I don't care as long as you guys are cooking. Well 1/3 of my sentence is almost done and I

Jacob Bradley

This is my special hug to you on Valentine's Day. I remember that you always liked Spongebob Square-pants, (and dad too). Who lives in a pineapple under the sea. There was a time when you said when you grew up you wanted to marry me, sound pretty funny now, huh. But you wanted to drive the yellow station wagon also. I hope you have a great day and hug Dad and Alexa for me

xxxo   Love Always Your Mom

think in 8 weeks or less I will be in Sioux Falls and it will be easier to see you and talk. I hope you are good to each other and I miss you more and more each day. Don't forget to call and go see grandma.

    I love you, Mary

Jacob Bradley,

    This is my special hug to you on Valentine's Day. I remember that you always liked SpongeBob Square Pants (and dad too). Who lives in a pineapple under the sea? There was a time when you said when you grew up you wanted to marry me, sounds pretty funny now, huh? But you wanted to drive the yellow station wagon also. I hope you have a great day and hug Dad and Alexa for me.

    xxxo Love Always, Your Mom

Journal Excerpt 26

20 January 2011 Day Fifty-Nine

There must be a full moon. Everyone is on edge. My roommate blew up because I spilled coffee on her shelf. A girl was upset because someone said I said something about her, which was untrue. Emotions are running rampant. Too many women too little space. A woman from work is saying I stink. Well my response was if she would work a little maybe she would sweat and stink too. Even I was drug into the drama. The key is to stay out of the way and try to avoid conflict. Good luck. Commissary came today so there is a lot of sugar and caffeine.

Journal Excerpt 27

29 January 2011 Day Sixty-Eight

I can't believe it has been so long since my last writing. Work has kept me tired and time goes fast.

17
Medical Isolation

Journal Excerpt 28

3 February 2011 Day Seventy-Three

On Tuesday I went to see the doctors at the clinic in Pierre. They had me see the surgeon instead and tested for MRSA. Today I was taken back to A-block for medical isolation. I was stripped of all my belongings and told nothing about what was going on. I don't know what MRSA is but I believe it is a serious permanent infection that will never be cured. I think I am having surgery tomorrow. I asked for a phone call but the guard keeps forgetting. It would be nice to call my husband and let him know about my medical condition.

The walls still have food and toilet paper stuck to them. The facility really needs a unit for the criminally insane, protective custody, and medical isolation separate from the people here for discipline reasons.

A fellow inmate was sent to A-block for refusing to work when she had a sore because she didn't want to catch MRSA. Now here I am. Why did they continue to make me work with dirty laundry with an open sore from a sliver, which eventually led to my contracting MRSA? Only the doctor was smart enough to give me a do not work order.

Journal Excerpt 30

4 February 2011 Day Seventy-Four

After surgery the doctor prescribed me medication and they put me back into the same filthy room without a hand towel or hot water to wash my hands. I am given a paper tray like I am on suicide watch.

Journal Excerpt 31

5 February 2011 Day Seventy-Five

Today they moved me to another room in A-block with no cable hookup so I only got to watch my TV that my brother bought, for 24 hours. They needed my room for a girl actually on suicide watch.

   The antibiotics are making me a little sick to my stomach and I remember the nurse at the hospital said I need to exercise a little. In fact, it was on the med order. I asked the nurse about it and she was very disagreeable. She said it is normal that it makes me sick but they don't order exercise in A-block.

5 February 2011

Hello lover,

   It was a big relief to hear from you this morning. I really can't imagine what all you have been going through. You are an extremely tough lady. You will need to apply that toughness to keeping your assorted demons at bay once you return home. I will do what I can to help because I fear that we, as a union, cannot survive the slightest backslide.

   I am very much looking forward to spending time with you, the real you, not the one that is subjugated by pride and indulgence. Well you are approaching the halfway mark. Stay strong, keep love in your heart, and know that you are never alone.

   Your loving husband, Brad

Journal Excerpt 32

6 February 2011 Day Seventy-Six

No information on MRSA has been given to me. I finally got to call

LISBETH, ANGLING
Carl Larsson
1853-1919

**Love and warm wishes
of the cheeriest kind
just to let you know
that you're on my mind!**

-Mom I miss you and love you deeply
I heard you got a bacteria I hope
you get well I love you so much

Jacob Giebink

-Mom I miss you and love you deeply
I heard you got a bacteria I hope
you get well I love you so much
Jacob Giebink

Brad. He was about to call the prison to see if I was alive and made it through surgery.

Journal Excerpt 33
7 February 2011 Day Seventy-Seven
I just got back from the doctor's and they ripped the Band-Aid off my finger with no reliever. We stopped at health services for aspirin. They said they would bring it to me but I bet they don't.

Journal Excerpt 34
9 February 2011 Day Seventy-Nine
I called Brad today. Talking to him makes me feel better.

Journal Excerpt 35
10 February 2011 Day Eighty
My finger has scabbed up and I should be out of here. I can't stop crying. I don't understand why they can't at least talk to me about what is going on.

12 February 2011
Hello lover,

I've enclosed some stuff-song lyrics, pictures. Glad you made it out of that nasty cell. That must be pure torment against your good hygiene sensibilities. The expenses are really piling up. We need to come up with a plan to cut back.

I just got off the phone with you and wish our talk had gone better. Please excuse me for being a little piqued at your critique of my conversational skills. I fully admit that I could do a lot better when it comes to conveying my thoughts to you and to listening patiently while you express your thoughts. It is just that I have this fresh memory of all the stuff that has come out of your mouth the last few years, and of how destructive it was to rely on what you said. I sure hope and pray that that is over with and that I will be able to put stock in what you say from here on out. For now, please show some forbearance of my touchiness. I wish you

well on your continued recovery. So much depends on it.
   Hugs and kisses, your husband

Journal Excerpt 36
14 February 2011 Day Eighty-Four
I got a short letter from John and a valentine from Jackie. Glad they care.

Journal Excerpt 37
16 February 2011 Day Eighty-Six
Signed up for domestic violence victim classes and chemical dependency treatment starting Tuesday.

16 February 2011
Dear Brad,
   I am writing this letter in A-block, the same room I was put in when they had me in a suicide gown. The room is filthy and disgusting. I don't believe it was cleaned since the last time I was here. They just told me I was going to have my surgery tomorrow morning and I probably will be in solitary confinement until my sore heals up. I am very scared. No one has told me anything except they had the guard tell me and everyone else that I have MRSA.
   I was supposed to pick up my TV today but I can't use it because I am in solitary confinement. They also wouldn't let me get my commissary. I wonder if I will have to do the antibiotic intravenously like I did when I had the problem with my elbow. I wish they would let me call you. I managed a quick call to Louis and I was pretty hysterical. I hope he called you to let you know what was going on. You would think that they could give me a sentence cut so I could go home to recuperate especially since the governor is looking at giving them anyways for inmates due to the budget cuts. I would love to send a letter to him but I don't have access to legal mail.
   I love you, Mary

Journal Excerpt 38
19 February 2011 Day Eighty-Nine
Yesterday I talked to my lawyer about a motion to cut my sentence; he is going to email the judge. The Attorney General's office will oppose it. I went to my doctors appoint February 17th. They were not pleased about my no show on the 10th. Health Services and the warden lied and said they didn't know about it.

Journal Excerpt 39
20 February 2011 Day Ninety
I went to Bible study with the Jehovah's Witnesses and watched a video about how they were persecuted by Hitler. It made the prison stay seem like a breeze, especially flashing back to my A-block stay.

Journal Excerpt 40
21 February 2011 Day Ninety-One
There is a lot of stealing going on. The bad girls are getting worse and threatening violence. I never respond to insults and walk away so I cannot escalate the problems. I think some people just like to fight or see a fight. I went to Bible study and it was perfect timing.

23 February 2011
Hello lover,

I think you are right about what we need to do. The ones we are most indebted to are our children. I normally think that a person should pay off all their debts. But in lieu of being able to do that, then it is most important to make up to those it matters to most. I have always intended to stay true to the spirit of our vows and don't plan on changing that course, now or ever.

Please take care and think about what we should do. Best wishes for success in your counseling and Bible studies.

Your loving husband, Brad

18
Released

At the end of February 2011 my mom started chemical dependency treatment. During treatment she wrote in a treatment journal that has now been lost, so we do not have journal entries from her for that time. However, she recalls it as an extremely helpful and productive time. For the first time my mom received information about alcoholism, the disease she suffered from. She also learned about triggers. Her counselor was excellent in getting to the heart of the problem and teaching the inmates how to stay sober once they were released.

The last session my mom attended the counselor tried to trigger my mom. "Mary, I've got this great weed. Why don't you light up the joint with me and smoke some? Come on, just a little." Although my mom knew it was her counselor saying this, she still got butterflies in her stomach. She was forced to think about how and why her previous behavior happened and how she could avoid it in the future. For example she needed to focus on permanently cutting ties with old 'friends,' forming new ways to cope with stress and reminding herself how her behavior affects the ones she loves.

My mom completed three out of the four weeks of treatment when she was suddenly transferred back to Sioux Falls towards the end of March. Her early release was not an issue because she had progressed enough in her treatment. There was an opening in the jail and my mom was allowed out on work release. The justice system might have been giving my mom a break. After applying for upwards of a hundred jobs, she was finally hired at Taco John's. Every day she rode a bicycle to work. It didn't matter that she was highly educated; the stigma of being a convict was overwhelming. It's a stigma that can be crippling to citizens trying to get back on their feet.

My mom was released from jail on May 8th, 2011. Although there was talk of her finding an efficiency unit, she moved in with us, in my childhood home. My parents' relationship had healed, not fully, but enough that it allowed them to live together and start rebuilding our lives.

In December 2011, after she was released, my mom was interviewed for an article in a local newspaper about picking yourself up after you fall. They quoted her saying, "Everything had to be taken away from me before I realized what I had. When I got to prison and my husband still loved me and my kids still loved me, that's when I realized what unconditional love was." Prison helped to transform my mom's behavior and attitude. She was stripped of everything with only our love remaining. This finally gave my mom the courage to sober up and start straightening her life out. Faith from her Bible studies and tools she learned in treatment allowed her to make progress then and continue her recovery now.

Epilogue

It has been about four and a half years since my mom was released from prison and from the chains of addiction and depression. Since then it has been a long slow walk upwards. My family has been working on repairing our relationships and figuring out how to interact healthily and productively. Sometimes it's very much a trial-and-error process. Surviving didn't make us perfect but we are more self-aware and truly want to make it work.

A main focus since my mom's release has been my brother, Jake. He was about 13 when she came home from prison and was on the precipice of those difficult teenager years. For a few years Jake worried us. He was lost and filled with angst just like Don. My mom tells me that my brother, Jacob, who is now 18, looks like Don. I see the resemblance when I look at pictures; both are tall, blond and have the round Galland head. The interesting thing is that my brother is also an artist. He loves to draw and sculpt. He hopes to one day go to art school but for now he is pursuing welding. Perhaps welding is an art for him.

It is common now, and in previous generations, for teenagers to have a hard time finding their way, especially if they associate with others who prove to be a bad influence. It was really hard for my parents and me to see my brother struggling. He was experimenting with drugs and alcohol. His interest in sports and hobbies was waning.

I worried that what had happened a few years before with my mother had adversely affected him. For me it had hardened my aversion to drugs and alcohol but I feared it had done the opposite for Jake. He was just so young. It was even harder for him than for me to understand what had happened and what was going on. Luckily, for some reason, he pulled through. For one, my parents never gave up. They supported him and tried at every step to help and understand although often he pushed back. He was going through the normal teenage issues with an added dose of tragedy and they knew that.

I also think that he was strong. As much as we wanted to control him, it was his choice to step away from the bad influences. His sophomore year my parents transferred him to another high school in the area. This gave him some distance from his bad associations, but it was still up to him to make the decision to hang out with them or not. Although harmful temptations are still strong and we all slip once in a while, he is on a path to success. He's on a path to happiness and health. Many of the boys he grew up with are now facing prison time for drug charges and more. Thankfully Jake escaped that fate. I love my brother so much, just like my mom loved her brother. I can't imagine losing Jake, like she lost Don.

When my mom was preoccupied with her addiction and imprisonment, I stepped in as a mother figure. I didn't do it consciously but Jake has since told me that he sees me as almost more of a mother figure than our mom. Perhaps this is why his irresponsible behavior worried me so much. When my mom was home again to parent, I had a hard time transitioning to the role of sister. I feel sometimes I am too hard on him, but I try to tell him I am immensely proud of him and love him more than anything. The responsibility I feel for Jake sounds similar to the responsibility my mom felt for her brother.

My parents did divorce but my mom never actually filed for bankruptcy. She has been working to make amends with creditors. Now, my mom is the Development Coordinator at the Glory House in Sioux

Falls. It is a facility where men and women can go after prison to receive treatment and support to get their lives back on track. Part of the proceeds from the sales of this book will go to the Glory House to help with their great work.

We all learned a lot going through the trials recounted in this book. My grandma likes to say, "Life is real and sometimes you have to live in it." In our lives we will face unbelievable circumstances that test the limits of our abilities. We do not have total control over how events will play out but we can do our best to navigate through them. Find support from family and friends that care about your wellbeing. Unconditional love is a powerful force. Find strength in faith and God if that is a source of comfort for you. I know that faith helped fortify both of my parents throughout the most difficult times, and continues to do so now.

One lesson my mom learned was humility. After prison, when she was working at Taco John's and then another fast food restaurant, Culver's, she had trouble at first accepting her position. To her, it seemed that she had fallen so far down, from owning a law firm to taking meal orders. Often men or women she knew from her time as a lawyer would come in and she would have the urge to run and hide. Eventually she stopped worrying about how she was reacting and started paying attention to the other person. Working at Taco John's was an honest job. She was meeting people, which she loves, and she was helping customers. It was time for her to be proud of herself and how far she had actually come, not how far she had fallen.

Another lesson my mom tries to be constantly aware of is the value of honesty. Before prison she lied and would tell people what she thought they wanted to hear. She lied because of shame and she lied because of fear. Being honest with yourself and others is freeing and it forms trust.

Lastly, we are all learning to forgive. For addicts to truly move on, they must forgive themselves in their hearts. There is a fear that nothing can replace drugs and alcohol but in reality you receive something much better. My mom considers herself a grateful recovering alcoholic. Because of her journey she has learned to look at life differently, more positively. She is learning to appreciate the love of others and the simply joys of life. However, one must not confuse forgiveness with forgetting. We must always be mindful of the past so that we do not repeat it. Every situation has a context and history.

I now have the words "Forgiveness is the ultimate form of love" tattooed in Latin on my ankle as a reminder to let go of the pain and frustration associated with my mom and her behavior. My role as a daughter is to love unconditionally and support her in recovery.

In prison my mom wasn't able to drink. The real test came when she was released. Her whole life she always felt in control. In her previous treatments many told her that alcoholics are powerless over their addiction. My mom saw herself as a powerful person and the thought of not being in control was ridiculous. Ultimately life did become unmanageable. She lost control.

When my mom was released from prison she began to gain some control back through surrendering and accepting. There are still weeks when she goes to AA five times, even though she has been sober for almost five years. Working at a treatment center has helped reinforce her knowledge of the disease and how to fight it. One of the most important struggles has been allowing herself to feel her emotions. She had her guard up for so long that it is hard still to let others know she is upset. It is a daily challenge for her and for us all.

Writing this book helped me understand what exactly my family went through, beginning with Don and continuing through my parents' story and Jake's and mine. It helped me process how we managed to survive. In writing this book I had many conversations with my family members, which helped us all move on even more. Talking about our issues truly is beneficial, even if it is five years afterwards.

I truly hope this book showed you that every family has its problems. No matter how perfect someone seems, they have their own demons. Although the impulse is strong to judge quickly, reach out a kind hand instead. Only through compassion and love can we overcome.